Gita on the GO

Aakriti has faced the same inner battles Arjuna did millennia ago, caught between ambition, pressure and uncertainty in a rapidly changing world. Standing at a personal crossroads in 2018 proved to be a turning point, when she discovered the transformative power of the Srimad Bhagavad Gita. What began as personal solace soon became a deeper calling, and inspired this book that sees the light of day five years later.

An MBA from IMT Ghaziabad with a background in marketing, Aakriti has worked with top brands like L'Oréal, Godrej and Noise. Yet beyond boardrooms and brand strategy, she sought something more enduring—a way to make sense of life's deeper questions. Her exploration led her to study the Gita alongside yogis, scholars and spiritual teachers, uncovering its relevance as a practical guide for modern living.

Today, she runs her own business and leads the Sevam Foundation, an NGO focused on equitable access to education and resources. She also shares her insights with a thoughtful community of over 60K followers on LinkedIn.

This book is not written from academic authority, but from experience—for anyone who's ever paused and asked 'what now' and longed for a grounded, compassionate answer.

Praise for the book

This book illuminates the striking relevance of the Bhagavad Gita for the modern era. It is like a mirror and a compass, reflecting our inner dilemmas while guiding us toward higher understanding. Through poignant stories drawn from the everyday lives of people grappling with pain, ego, duty, and doubt, the author skilfully reveals the essence of Lord Krishna's teachings—not amidst Kurukshetra, but within the silent warzones of our own minds.

Each chapter reminds us that true worth is not found in how many challenges we conquer externally, but by how courageously we face our inner chaos. The narrative inspires the reader to rise above reaction, to act with detachment, to love selflessly, to give without discrimination and to serve with humility.

My heartfelt congratulations to the author for distilling divine wisdom into a form that speaks powerfully to the modern seeker. My best wishes to all the readers—not only to understand the teachings of the Gita, but to embody them, and to live with greater awareness, equanimity and purpose.

—Swami Mukundananda, Founder, JKYog

Aakriti Bansal narrates the application of the Gita through the characters in the book. Easy to read, the book helps us relate to the people in the story as if they are our own dilemmas and real-life situations. Read on to understand the confused Arjuna in you being guided to find solutions to modern-day problems.

—Dr Radhakrishnan Pillai,
speaker and author of *Corporate Chanakya*

Aakriti has done a wonderful job in bridging Shreemad Gita with the newer. This book shall be a good start point to many and in the process would have successfully implanted a thirst in people to read Gita and its profound meanings.

—Anand Pillai, mentor and wanderer

Gita on the GO

AAKRITI BANSAL

Published by
Rupa Publications India Pvt. Ltd 2025
161-B/4, Gulmohar House,
Yusuf Sarai Community Centre,
New Delhi 110049

Sales centres:
Bengaluru Chennai
Hyderabad Kolkata Mumbai

Copyright © Aakriti Bansal 2025

This is a work of fiction. Names, characters, places and incidents are either the product of the author's imagination or are used fictitiously and any resemblance to any actual person, living or dead, events or locales is entirely coincidental.

All rights reserved.

No part of this publication may be reproduced, transmitted, or stored in a retrieval system, in any form or by any means, electronic, mechanical, photocopying, recording or otherwise, without the prior permission of the publisher.

P-ISBN: 978-93-7003-426-6
E-ISBN: 978-93-7003-172-2

Third impression 2025

10 9 8 7 6 5 4 3

The moral right of the author has been asserted.

Printed in India

This book is sold subject to the condition that it shall not, by way of trade or otherwise, be lent, resold, hired out, or otherwise circulated, without the publisher's prior consent, in any form of binding or cover other than that in which it is published.

Contents

1. *Prarambh*: The First Step / 1
2. *Chintan*: The Mirror / 28
3. *Vivek*: Truth vs Illusion / 42
4. *Mukti*: Breaking Free / 57
5. *Nishkām*: Action without Fruit / 70
6. *Samatol*: The Balance / 88
7. *Sankalp*: Purpose Overcomes Fear / 97
8. *Prakash*: Light Within / 113
9. *Nishchay*: Steadfast Within / 125
10. *Anitya*: This Too Shall Pass / 139
11. *Purnahuti*: A Return to Self / 148

Author's Note / 163

1
Prarambh: The First Step

I am Arjuna. And my mind is the battlefield of Kurukshetra.

One phone call changed everything. When I heard him cry through the phone, followed by the doctor's terse prescription, it hit me like a storm I hadn't seen coming. Without a second thought, I abandoned my schedule, made some calls and just jumped into action to book the earliest flight home.

My mind was in complete chaos.

I glanced down at my wristwatch: 9:15 a.m. A wave of panic surged through me as I realized I might miss my flight. I hurriedly checked out of the hotel and rushed into the waiting cab that I had asked the reception to book for me.

I hadn't even begun to process what was happening. All I could focus on was making it to the airport in time. My son needed me.

Breathless, with my heart pounding so loud in my chest that it echoed in my ears, I dashed through the airport gates.

I elbowed my way to the front of the queue to collect my boarding pass, ignoring the annoyed glances and muttered insults thrown my way for breaking the line. At this moment in time, I didn't care.

'Ma'am, your flight has been delayed by two hours. We apologize for the inconvenience,' the check-in attendant casually mentioned after I rattled out my booking details.

Delayed! The word hit me like a slap. The words then flew out raw and sharp. 'Is this all a joke to you? Are your flights ever on time? I need to get to my son who is not well. Please find me another flight. Now. Or I shall sue you and your airline,' I blurted out. I didn't stop to weigh my words; they simply erupted without a second thought, fuelled by desperation and a mother's rising fury.

My little outburst had drawn an audience. The hushed curses from the queue behind me had dissolved into a heavy silence. I could feel the weight of about twenty pairs of eyes on my back but I could see only one face—my son. He needed me.

'I'm sorry, ma'am. All the flights are delayed due to the weather. Yours will be the first to board once the weather clears. I understand that you are in a hurry but there's really nothing we can do right now,' the attendant said gently but firmly.

Before I could unleash another round of helpless desperation in words, the attendant gave me a tight, practised, dismissive smile. I understood. It was my cue to exit.

I turned around and started walking towards the security check, every step heavy with frustration at not having any other option.

As I reached into my handbag, fumbling for the small bottle of water to calm my nerves, my hands trembled.

As I headed towards the boarding gate with the security check completed, the handbag slipped from my grip onto the floor, scattering its contents like my thoughts—messy, out of place and far too many. My frustration only increased.

'Of course,' I muttered under my breath. Everything just has to go wrong today. Why today, the one day I need everything to go right? I thought to myself as I bent down to gather my things which now lay spread on the floor.

As I clumsily began to shove my belongings back into my handbag, I noticed another pair of hands alongside mine, gently gathering some of the items. I looked up, startled, and met the kind eyes of a man who had stopped to help.

'Are you okay? You seem a little distressed,' he asked, his voice laced with genuine concern.

'I just...' I couldn't even complete my sentence. I could barely breathe, let alone explain. Nothing made sense in that instant.

'Here, take a moment, calm down. Would you like some water?' he asked softly, offering me a bottle of water.

'No, thank you,' I nodded and managed to force a faint smile. 'I really appreciate your help but I am a little distraught. My flight's been delayed by two hours and I just can't wait that long. Not today,' I responded, still distraught.

'Which flight are you on?' he asked, taking a peek at my boarding pass.

'Hey, I am on the same flight to Delhi too. The flight's been delayed by two hours due to anticipated storms. No other flights will be flying out either. Not in this weather.'

Prarambh: The First Step • 3

I just looked at him. I could understand nothing. I heard but could not comprehend. All I could think about was my son—his soft voice asking for me.

'Are you kidding? Two hours?' I burst out.

'Hey, it's alright. You mentioned you can't be late today. Any urgent business you need to attend to? If you don't mind me asking,' he enquired carefully.

I was a little vexed by all the questions though I knew he meant well.

'My son is sick. I need to be with him,' I answered quietly.

He nodded. 'I understand. My mother, even today, worries when I'm sick. Calls me a dozen times a day, no matter how much I assure her that I'll be fine or there is family who is there to help,' he said.

I could sense he was trying to comfort me, but his words were like water off a duck's back. I was too immersed in myself and my need to be with my little one.

Finding myself at a loss for words, I just nodded with a weak smile.

'Your son will be just fine,' he responded. 'The universe works in mysterious ways. Maybe this delay is a blessing in disguise,' he added, with a knowing smile.

Exasperation surged through me. How could this delay be for the better? Stranded at the airport, miles from my sick son who needs his mother? How could this man possibly suggest that there could be a silver lining? I thought to myself.

Sweat dripped down my face. My chest tightened and I could feel myself gasping for air but each breath felt harder than the last. The constant buzz of the airport terminal, the announcements about flight delays, the rolling suitcases, people all around me, their murmuring voices—all of it felt like a crushing weight on me. I felt suffocated.

I did not reply and started rushing towards the gate, my thoughts spiralling and my mind consumed with the urgency of this journey.

The man naturally followed behind me, as we were after all on the same flight.

I felt foolish for not anticipating the delay caused by the weather, and guilt set in. How could I miss something this basic? Had I thought of this in time, I probably would have spared myself the growing anger, worry and helpless frustration.

We finally sank into the seats near the boarding gate, sitting side by side in an uneasy silence. I was lost in my thoughts, my long coat slightly damp from the rain. Perhaps I could call the doctor and seek an update on my son's health. Consumed with texting the doctor from my phone and checking for updates, hoping for good news, I paid almost zero attention to the kind stranger sitting quietly beside me.

'Mumma's going to be there soon,' I whispered to myself in my head, like a quiet promise, a mantra I needed to believe.

Yet within this internal and external disarray, just the presence of the stranger I had just met steadied the chaos and gave me a sense of security. Soon, I felt oddly grounded by his calm.

As my inner voices quietened down, something compelled me to focus my attention on this stranger. He was unlike anyone I'd ever encountered at an airport.

He was tall, with long, curly hair that tumbled down to his shoulders. He was dressed in loose white pants and a yellow kurta with a dark yellow overcoat. Traditional yet modern. His appearance was striking yet serene. His hair cascaded down to his shoulders and his deep-set eyes were bright and shiny—like tiny sapphires holding a quiet kindness.

Weirdly, when he had first spoken to me amid my turmoil, he had greeted me with a sweet, honey-like voice. As our conversation replayed in my mind, I felt a twinge of regret at not having acknowledged his patience and kindness to me. I owed him better.

I cleared my thoughts and turning to him greeted him again, 'Thank you for helping me. I couldn't completely thank you before.'

I half expected him to nod or maybe say it was nothing, which would conclude the conversation.

Little did I know then that this was the beginning of my conversation with 'Kannan'.

♦

'How old is your son?' he asked.

'Eight,' I replied.

'And there is no one to take care of him?' he enquired further.

I caught myself wondering whether I should really be entertaining so many intrusive questions from a complete stranger. It went against my instincts. My hesitation must have been quite evident, as he quickly continued with a smile, without missing a beat.

'Silly of me to ask you so many questions directly without even introducing myself. Let's rewind a little. I am Kannan. I am a psychologist at Safdarjung Hospital and lecture as a professor at Delhi University. I also have a daughter who is 10 years old and the light of our lives.'

'That's sweet,' I smiled back and eased into the conversation. 'That explains why you could understand my distress,' I added.

'Speaking of which, is there no one to take care of him?' he enquired.

His persistence may have annoyed me under different circumstances, but his tone was kind and I felt safe. He was not trying to seek information from me; he was reaching out to me. Moreover, in all honesty, we were stuck at the airport for the next two hours and with my nerves already stretched paper-thin, a distraction was exactly what I needed. So I let my walls down and obliged him with a response.

'My mom is there,' I said politely.

'Then why were you in such a hurry?' he questioned.

It seemed a surprisingly relevant question. I thought to myself for a minute or two and replied, 'He needs me. This is the first time since he was born that I have not been there for him. He has been diagnosed with jaundice; he was vomiting all morning. I am afraid his condition might deteriorate without me being there.'

'Have you spoken with him today?'

'Yes.'

'How did he sound?' Kannan probed.

'He sounded okay although he did say he wanted me to come home soon,' I said, puzzled, not knowing where the conversation was leading.

'So what would you have done differently had the flight not been delayed and you had reached your child earlier?'

The question caught me off guard. I was taken aback. It seemed as if a stone had dropped into still water, small, yet sending out ripples far and wide.

I hadn't even considered that my mom was there with Aryan. My mom had raised me with love and care. She was also there for Aryan when I went to work. He wasn't alone. He was safe. Why did I feel like I needed to be home right now? I had not expected Kannan to ask this question so bluntly.

And then it struck me. Why did I not think of it like that?

It was my own fear and guilt; my spiralling anxiety about being helpless which had pushed me to this point. The situation at home did not demand my presence on an immediate basis; it was all in my head. It was just my urgent desire to be with my son even though I couldn't have done anything different from what my mom was already doing.

I fell silent. I realized how my desire to be with my son and fear of him getting sicker were both delusions of my mind that had had a ripple effect on all my actions today—rushing for my flight while underestimating the bad weather, demanding answers, lashing out at the attendant, being visibly upset with the situation, then blaming the weather and the delayed flight for my suffering.

Still somewhat fearful, I prayed that a delay of a couple of hours wouldn't matter as my mom was already with him. Either way we had to observe him for a day to check if the prescribed medicines were working.

I also realized how impulsively I had been reacting lately, not just today. Could it be because I was trying too hard to keep busy after the divorce, not wanting to think about how my life was changing in the big picture?

Kannan sensed from my silence how the weight of his question had provoked me to think deeper. Maybe that was what he wanted—not to question, but guide. Hold up a mirror to help me become aware about my actions in the bigger play, that I was too overwhelmed to notice.

♦

Kannan watched with a knowing smile, his sapphire-like eyes radiating an ancient wisdom that seemed to transcend time and space. 'The Universe has its own language and whispers to us through signs and symbols, through patterns, unexpected encounters, or even delays. It guides us,' he said almost as if he were speaking to the wind. 'Nudging us towards our destiny, helping us to learn important lessons. You just need to keep yourself calm and open to be able to see it.'

'Have you ever found yourself fielding similar problems time and again? Like getting betrayed by people or falling sick again and again?' he asked.

'Yes, but what is it with the same kinds of problems? Can I not have variety even there?' I mocked my situation.

'Well, here is how the Universe works in my opinion. It keeps throwing the same set of problems at you till you really learn the lesson intended for you. The Universe is like "oh, she did not learn even this time? I guess she'll have to do it all over again." Just like we used to redo our homework if we got something wrong. It's simple. If you are falling sick repeatedly, for instance, maybe you are not learning to take care of your body,' he said.

I listened intently, feeling a sense of awe at the newness of his words that compelled me to think deeper. For far too long, I had been caught up in my own small problems, blinded to the nuances of my immediate environment, living only on the surface. Not trying to go deeper or check to see if there was a bigger lesson for me in there. But now this stranger who I met minutes ago was somehow offering me some perspective. Even if it was temporary, I realized that I had been craving this clarity. It was what I needed.

'It intrigues me how we create our own problems,' he continued, his voice low and melodic. 'We get caught up in our own patterns of thinking and behaviours and end up repeatedly creating roadblocks for ourselves,' he said.

His words stung me and my expression tightened. 'What is that supposed to mean?' I asked, clearly displeased. I felt invalidated. Did he think my problem was not genuine? How was being away from my son when he was sick a problem I chose to create? My mind refused to accept his statement.

As I wrestled with my thoughts, he reached into his bag and pulled out a small, leather-bound notebook. Without saying a word, he flipped it open and started to write down something. I stared at Kannan with a mix of disbelief and irritation bubbling within me. How could he make a statement which triggered and provoked me at all possible levels, clearly perceive my discomfort and then decide to doodle in his diary? I fumed.

Who is he? I thought.

My mind raised a storm of thoughts, leaping from confusion to curiosity to annoyance, from one extreme emotion to another, with scarcely any moment to process even one of them completely.

Then without any warning, Kannan looked at me and

spoke again. 'Don't misunderstand me. I am not undermining your situation; being far away from someone you love, especially when they are unwell. But sometimes we need to reframe the moment to survive it. Here, let me explain this. Whenever I am stuck, I try to analyse the situation through a communication concept called SCQA, which is Situation, Complication, Question and Analysis, a process widely used by business consultants like McKinsey, Boston Consulting Group (BCG) and Bain. I frequently include this topic even in my lectures and students find it very useful, especially in times of crisis,' he smiled as he said this.

I stared at him, completely lost, until Kannan continued to explain his concept.

'Let's take an example,' he began.

'Imagine this. My wife and I want to move the family into a larger house. But my parents are not on board with this plan because they do not want to change their routine or their circle of friends in our neighbourhood. For them, moving out would mean losing their world. What should I do?' He paused before continuing.

It seemed like a rhetorical question but I still started anticipating answers. However, before I could speak, he continued.

'This method can be used for clarity to emerge when navigating problems like this. As per the SCQA concept, we break down this conundrum into three components—situation, complication and question—and then we analyse it.'

He turned his notebook towards me, letting me see what he had been working on. I noticed he had created a table on the page and divided the facts of the conflict into the exact three components he had mentioned, besides adding some questions and remarks under each section.

'Here, let me show you,' he said.

Situation	We need a bigger house.
Complication	We need a larger space to meet the growing needs of the family but my parents don't want to move. They have an existing friends circle in our locality and are reluctant to change their routine.
Question	Is the bigger house absolutely necessary? Can it wait for some time? What emotional significance does this neighbourhood hold for my parents? Are we ready to accept that?

'If I were to answer these questions, let's see where we arrive.

1. Yes, we have a daughter who needs her own room. She is growing up and demands privacy.
2. She is eight years old, so she can wait for two more years.
3. It is important because we are all busy with work, so their friends often become their only outlet for social contact.
4. Yes. We need to. I am sure we can manage.

'After looking at the questions and answers, we decided that yes, we needed a larger house in the same neighbourhood, but not immediately. We have two years to locate a suitable house. Are you able to follow?' Kannan asked.

I nodded.

'Now, let's do an analysis of your situation through SCQA. Here, take my diary,' he said as he handed the notebook to me. I started writing the following:

Situation	My son is ill.
Complication	I am unable to be with him due to flight delays and bad weather conditions.
Question	Would it make a difference if I reached earlier? Would it really matter if I reached two-three hours late? Why did I want to reach my son early?

I handed him the diary, patiently waiting for him to read what I had written. He looked pleased. His eyes started to glow with quiet satisfaction and a slight smile curled at the edges of his lips.

'Now answer these for me, please,' he asked, handing the diary back to me.

I knew this was coming. I started writing down the answers—not giving it much thought. I simply wrote whatever came to me first; instinct over deliberation.

1. No. My mom is taking good care of my son.
2. No. My mom is already there.
3. To curb personal guilt and attain peace of mind.

As I wrote the last sentence, I raised my head from the notebook to look at Kannan in disbelief. I wanted peace of mind, yet that was the very thing I had disrupted most during this journey. That in turn had created a ripple effect on every incident that unfolded.

Pleased with my effort, I handed the diary back to Kannan to read my answers. Uncannily, he refused to look.

'I already know what you might have written,' he said calmly. 'Your eyes reveal more than you think. Here's what I want you to understand: when we become aware of our personal tendencies, patterns or mental responses, we begin to change. For change to happen, we must first become self-aware. Awareness is the seed. Then we must begin to acknowledge situations and facts. For example, if you are self-aware, even if someone provokes you, you'd recognize your urge to burst into anger and curse—but instead, you may consciously choose to pause, refrain from an outburst and if possible, avoid having that conversation, or respond differently, especially if others aren't receptive.'

I nodded, as the truth in his words started to sink in. 'I guess lately I have been getting irritated by even the slightest inconveniences,' I admitted. 'A lot has been going on in my life and even minor problems seem to trigger a chain reaction that's hard to curtail.'

The awareness was there, but I could neither fully accept it aloud, nor change it immediately. Was this how it was supposed to be? I wanted to ask Kannan, but hesitation held me back.

Kannan smiled, as if sensing my inner conflict. 'Perhaps this delay is a blessing disguised as an inconvenience. Isn't that a possibility? Have you ever considered that suffering might bring a unique blessing or impart a valuable learning?'

I stared at him, puzzled and unconvinced. 'How exactly is being stranded at the airport a blessing?' I asked, my frustration slowly creeping back.

He chuckled softly as though he had anticipated this question. And he was ready for it. 'Look at it this way. Perhaps it's giving you an opportunity to slow down and reflect on your journey, not just the physical one but the inner one too; or think of the things you've been ignorant to. Maybe it's a sign for you to look at things from a different perspective.'

His words were forcing me to think from a completely new angle. They tugged at something deep within me—something I had been neglecting for far too long. After my separation from my husband, I had been so busy putting together the pieces of my life that I had forgotten to slow down, pause and reflect. I had been focused on building the frame, but I'd ignored the foundation.

The lesson had been right in front of me all along. Yet somehow I hadn't been able to see it in its entirety. It would take courage to look a little deeper.

◆

As I closed the notebook and handed it back to him, Kannan pulled out another book from his bag and flipped it open to a marked passage. 'Listen to this,' he said.

uddhared atmanatmanam natmanam avasadayet
atmaiva hy atmano bandhur atmaiva ripur atmanah

I could not understand the words he said and stared at him cluelessly. I knew it was Sanskrit but couldn't understand what it meant or how it was relevant to our conversation. By this point, I figured that everything Kannan did felt enigmatic but with patience the mist would clear.

Kannan, being perceptive, saw the doubt and announced, 'Shree Bhagavad Gita, Chapter 6, Verse 5.'

I nodded as if I knew all about it. Of course I had heard of the Bhagavad Gita, but it had never made it to my reading list.

'Do you understand what that means?' Kannan enquired playfully, fully aware that I didn't.

'I'd be lying if I said I did,' I admitted, embarrassed at my ignorance. 'But why the sudden mention?' I enquired.

Kannan continued, his voice steady, almost meditative, as if he had not heard me.

'Let a man lift himself by himself; let him not degrade himself. For the self alone is the friend of oneself and the self alone is the enemy of oneself.' He paused as if allowing me to breathe in the essence of these words.

'*Uddhared* means to elevate. *Avasadayet* means to degrade. It means that it is our mind that either elevates us by helping us realize our actual selves or degrades us by taking us away from it. Our mind can be our greatest ally, or our fiercest enemy. So, we need to find who we really are. And finding the self is not about reaching a destination. It is all about the journey.

'To truly understand the self, one must practise consistent self-enquiry, observing thoughts and feelings with calm detachment—free of judgement and effort; just introspection.

The journey of self-awareness is not about achieving a final state but being fully present and aware in each moment, recognizing the conditioned responses of the mind and seeing beyond them.'

As I sat there in contemplation, some of it started to make sense. However, I had a follow-up question that I blurted out candidly, 'But Kannan, we always think we are right. No one ever says they are wrong. That is how the brain functions, right?'

He smiled and said, 'That is not how the brain functions. It is how the ego works. To truly introspect, we must let go of our ego and rationalize. We always know when we are wrong. It is just our perceived notions and ego that do not let us accept it.'

I was amazed at how Kannan had summed up a powerful message so beautifully in one sentence. Kannan remained quiet, letting me absorb the truth.

'You know, Kannan, I have always longed for a mentor and kept reaching out to people hoping they could give me some direction and clarity on my life. Someone who could tell me things just like you have. What I didn't realize was that it was sitting right there on my study desk at home. I never imagined that the Shree Bhagavad Gita echoes learning in such a powerful and thought-provoking manner,' I said.

'It's timeless,' Kannan simply smiled with these words.

♦

While I sat deep in thought, retracing the events since morning, the attendant announced, 'Flight A203 from Mumbai to Delhi, now boarding.'

We both got up and headed to the boarding gate.

I thought then that the conversation with Kannan would end and we would part ways into our regular lives. The thought saddened me. There was so much more that I wanted to know and learn. I had not met anyone yet who could compel me to think differently.

But what could I have done?

I turned to Kannan with gratitude.

'Thank you so much for helping me place the situation in perspective. I feel lighter. I shall remember today for the rest of my life,' I said as I bid farewell to him.

He smiled. 'I am glad I could help,' he said as we headed towards the gate.

Little did I know then that the Universe had plans of its own.

♦

On the aircraft, just as I settled into my seat, I saw Kannan walking up the aisle. To my absolute surprise, he walked up to my row and occupied the seat next to mine. He was going to be my co-passenger! I was thrilled. Was this a sign from the Universe answering my silent wish?

'Well, well, so we meet again,' he said, his eyes twinkling. 'It seems our conversation isn't over just yet,' he said with a teasing smile.

As the engines roared to life and the flight took off, our conversation flowed once more, unhurried and thought-provoking.

♦

'So let me ask you another question. Do you find yourself stuck in a loop, often battling difficult situations and weighed down by negativity, convinced that life is full of obstacles?' he asked.

His statement resonated with me and without a thought, I exclaimed, 'Yes!'

'I observe people for a living. And I have noticed that society has hardwired us to believe that struggle is a natural part of life, without which we cannot fully appreciate life. I am sure you have heard the phrase "you must have bad days to appreciate the good ones".'

'Absolutely,' I agreed, nodding. 'Yes, I have heard of it,' I said, finally feeling some satisfaction that for a change I understood what he was saying.

'Now what if I were to tell you that it is these problems that are blocking us from experiencing happiness?' Kannan asked.

I was quite confused, but having started to know him a little, I knew he was heading to a tangent. So I played along.

'Isn't that obvious?' I enquired.

'It is. But what if I told you that we deliberately *create* problems on our own?'

'That's ridiculous. You mentioned this earlier at the boarding gate too. Why would anyone who is not an idiot do that? Who would deliberately create problems for themselves. It's like walking into a rainstorm and complaining about getting wet.' As I spoke out loud, I caught some peculiar stares from neighbouring passengers. Embarrassed, I mellowed down.

Prarambh: The First Step • 19

'What if I were to tell you that we create these problems unknowingly?' He stood by his question.

'Why would we sabotage ourselves like that?' I asked, bewildered by his bizarre question.

'Let me explain this more clearly. I'm guessing you've heard of the concept of "stimuli" before—these are the external factors that trigger us to respond. Throughout our lives, we require certain motivations or catalysts—whether that's encouragement, challenge or even pressure—to maintain our momentum and drive us forward. Just like a car that needs fuel to run. Does this make sense to you, that we often need an external nudge to stay motivated?'

'Yes,' I said, intrigued.

'What if I told you that our minds, when without a stimulus or a goal to chase, start to create problems in response to the anxiety that arises in the absence of immediate stimuli?

'Over the years, our minds have developed a powerful association between solving problems and creating value. Think of it like this: when we successfully tackle a challenge—whether it's fixing something broken, resolving a conflict or overcoming an obstacle—we experience immediate satisfaction and can point to concrete results. These solutions provide us with clear evidence of our competence and worth.

'However, when our lives lack pressing crises or urgent problems to solve, we feel at a loose end. Without immediate issues demanding our attention, we're forced to confront much deeper, unsettling questions about our existence. Questions like "What am I truly doing with my life?" or "Where am I actually headed?" emerge from the quiet spaces. Unlike practical problems with straightforward solutions, these existential questions don't offer quick answers or measurable outcomes. They require sustained reflection and often bring considerable discomfort as they challenge our fundamental assumptions about ourselves and our purpose.

'So, without purpose, we subconsciously create new problems to feel like heroes. We often associate our sense of self-worth with the sheer number of problems we can solve. The more fires we put out, the more valued we feel.'

I leaned back, stunned. I had never perceived this angle before. It was too much to digest in one go. Yet it made sense. If I were to think rationally, I too had created problems for myself today. Like snapping irritably at the attendant. It wasn't necessary but wasn't it my way of feeling that I was taking action in reaching my son?

'So does this pattern have a ripple effect on other aspects of life?' I asked.

'Of course it does,' he replied promptly. 'In the long run, we end up sabotaging relationships, procrastinating tasks and sowing seeds of self-doubt—one adverse outcome and it all comes crashing down.'

'And we are doing all this just because we're bored?' I asked with child-like innocence.

He smiled.

'You could say that, although I would replace the word bored with ignorant.'

There was no winning with Kannan—he was always ready with an answer and had a way with words.

He then quoted from the Gita.

prakriteḥ kriyamāṇāni guṇaiḥ karmāṇi sarvaśaḥ
ahankaarae-vimūḍhātmā kartāham iti manyate

Chapter 3, Verse 27

'It says that one who is ignorant, the one with ego, identifies himself as the doer, thinking that he enables everything in his world.

'Our ego is a paradox, a double-edged sword. On one hand, it propels us to pursue our goals and dreams and feel accomplished when we succeed. Yet it is also a trickster that binds us in a cycle of self-imposed problems—with which we struggle and suffer—and leads us down the path of self-destruction. Thus making us even more ignorant to the true nature of *Atma*[1]—the pure untouched Self beneath all our stories and striving.

'Sometimes, the ego craves chaos and can lead us to create problems solely for the satisfaction of solving them, obtaining gratification or even to seek attention and sympathy as a victim. As a master illusionist, the ego can cast us as both the creator or the victim of our own narrative.'

'I don't follow. You mentioned ego earlier as well. But fundamentally, my ego is a part of me, right? How do I separate from it?' I asked curiously.

'Let me give you an example. Priyam, a manager at a tech firm, had a reputation for being highly competent. When he hired Rupal, a brilliant new team member, his

---

[1] In Hindu philosophy, Atma—the inner essence of oneself— is translated as the 'Self' distinct from the body and mind. It is characterized by consciousness, free will and ethical awareness.

initial intention was to use her ideas to boost sales. But soon he started to feel threatened. Though he wouldn't admit it consciously, her enthusiasm challenged his own self-image as the department's most competent person. His ego couldn't tolerate this perceived challenge to his status. Rather than collaborating with Rupal, Priyam began to subtly undermine her and her ideas. He would point out flaws in her proposals during meetings, "accidentally" exclude her from important email chains and even take credit for her ideas in conversations with the senior leadership. He started to create unnecessary hurdles for her projects and questioned her decisions even when they aligned with the company's best practices.

'His team's morale deteriorated, as did his reputation—from a "competent manager" to an "insecure obstacle". His ego prevented him from recognizing that he had manufactured conflict where collaboration would have benefited everyone—including himself. Priyam created significant workplace problems simply because his ego couldn't accept that someone else might shine brightly without diminishing his own value and status.'

Kannan continued, 'Ultimately, it is upon us to recognize how our ego moulds our thinking, to better understand why we behave the way we do. To really understand this, we need to look at what is ego. Ego isn't our true self—it's more like a made-up version of who we think we are, built up over time. It's the belief that we're fully in charge of everything we do and everything that happens to us. As we grow up and focus more on material things like money, success and status, we start thinking that we can control everything in our lives. And this is where the actual problem begins.

'The ego convinces us that we are separate, independent people rather than interconnected beings influenced by myriad factors beyond our control, like the actions of other people, luck or even the environment. When we identify too strongly with this false self, of being separate or exerting control, we become trapped in similar patterns of behaviour that ultimately create problems not only for us, but also for others. The journey inward, to know the "Self", is not meant to conquer the ego but to see through its disguise. This reminds me of another verse from the Bhagavad Gita,' Kannan said as he paused. He then quoted:

Bandhur atmatmanas tasya yenatmaivatmana jitah
Anatmanas tu satrutve vartetatmaiva satru-vat

Chapter 6, Verse 6

For one who has conquered the mind, the mind is the best of friends; but for one who has failed to do so, his mind will remain the greatest enemy.

'Wait, now I'm confused. Why don't we realize what is happening?' I asked.

'Valid question and exactly what one should be asking. But to answer that I'll need to explain a concept to you. Power through.

'Life can throw two types of crises our way:

Sudden	Gradual
When hit with a sudden crisis, we usually react quickly to address it in a fight or flight response.	When a crisis builds up slowly, we often fail to recognize it until it is too late. We then feel we have no control over the situation and stop trying to change it even when there are opportunities to do so. The psychologist Martin E.P. Seligman first explained this concept of learned helplessness in the 1960s.

Before we dig deeper, have you heard of the boiling frog syndrome?'

'No,' I said, realizing how little I knew.

'Well, if you place a frog in water at room temperature, it's fine. If you gradually raise the temperature of the water, it does not notice and fails to comprehend the changing environment until it eventually boils to death,' Kannan explained and paused.

By now, I understood that Kannan was not one to provide straight answers—he built concept upon concept and question on question. I was absolutely perplexed now. I had many thoughts that seemed too much to consume at once.

Sensing my confusion, he elaborated, 'Let me walk you through this. We become so used to prolonged struggles that we become comfortable and learn to work around these problems. We cannot imagine life without the suffering. We even create new problems to maintain the familiar environment of stress, thus falling prey to the "boiling frog syndrome"—adjusting to rising temperatures until it's too late.

'This isn't just about individuals—it's everywhere. Entire organizations have fallen into this trap. Two companies, Kodak and Polaroid, clung to the familiarity of outdated technology and business models, failing to recognize the gradual innovation and competitive threats in their industry until a newer player swooped in and stole their market share. We must learn to recognize the gradual crises and at the same time embrace change. Breaking free from learned helplessness or the gradual changes that obviously do not come with warning signs, to take charge of our situation means stepping out of our comfort zone, but ultimately leads to a healthier, focused mind.'

My mind was whirling. I sat there absorbing the weight of his words. 'It's a lot to digest, even though I can grasp some of it,' I said.

He laughed. 'You are not meant to understand all of it in one go. No one does. Humans are so complex with their unique conditioning, beliefs and identity that it would take years to untangle all of it. However, the good news is you just need to recognize the patterns to break free. This means first you must have the awareness that there is a pattern. To be able to identify the pattern, you need to introspect and let go of your ego. Step two is critical. You need to accept that your own habit may be feeding your frustration that leads you to constant challenges. If you don't know or cannot accept that a problem exists, how would you solve it? But that is another discussion. Just start with introspection for now. Go deeper, ask the uncomfortable questions, and be willing to see a pattern.'

As he said this, the pilot announced that we would soon be landing. I simply smiled, pulled down my eye mask and dozed off for the next half hour to allow it all to sink in.

Aren't we all Arjuna? Our mind is a battlefield where the conflicts of desires, fears and thoughts wage a war.

2
Chintan: The Mirror

As Pragya dragged herself out of bed and slid the curtains open, sunlight surged in to light up her room, hitting her face with its full intensity. She winced, squinting. Involuntarily, her fingers flew to her face, feeling the tightness of her cheeks, the tough texture.

She was already dreading the day as she had another counselling session scheduled with yet another psychologist. For her they were all the same, repeating rehearsed lines, trying to get her to move on. What do they know? she thought to herself.

'Ma, where have you kept my green suit?' she shouted from her room while drying herself after a cool shower. She needed to calm her weary nerves before the arrival of this new psychologist. After the shocking event, her parents had urged her towards therapy. They had arranged several sessions for her at home with different counsellors, but none could help her. She remained homebound, lacking the courage to go out and face the world. This psychologist though—Kannan, her mother had informed her—was known to try off-book therapies for personal growth. He arrived on time.

Kannan sat across from Pragya in the living room of her house in a small town called Hapur, 80 kilometres from Delhi, in Uttar Pradesh, and away from the hustle-bustle of the main town. Her two-storey home, with its single cramped bedroom upstairs, offered little escape from the heat even with breeze flowing in from the half-open window.

Kannan studied Pragya in silence before carefully speaking in a deliberate voice, 'Tell me, Pragya, what do you think has been the hardest part of your journey?'

This question triggered a relentless wave of painful memories. To her surprise, however, this psychologist had not started the conversation with polite questions like 'how do you feel today?' or 'have you been keeping well?' Yet, what he had asked her was actually tougher.

Kannan could sense this was a difficult question for Pragya and so he sat still, waiting, to give her the time she needed.

Pragya closed her eyes and took a deep breath, steadying herself against the rush of emotional pain that the question stirred.

I wish there was a single answer. I'd be grateful for that, she thought. Her life had been a relentless series of battles over the last three years. The judgements of people she knew followed her like a shadow, not just in the courtrooms but even in her own home. Her gaze drifted through the window to the sky; the calm outside seemed in contrast to the storm raging within her.

'Acceptance,' she finally said, in a low voice. 'Accepting what has happened to me, accepting my new reality, how my life has changed and what it has become. That's been the hardest part.'

Kannan nodded silently, his eyes kind with empathy. He knew there was more.

'It's not like I don't want to move on, but people don't let me forget, not even for a moment. Even my own family looks at me mostly with pity, and sometimes anger. They have had to go through so much because of what happened to me,' she continued.

'I am sure it has been difficult,' Kannan agreed, letting her continue.

'Yes, it has. I understand what people say or think should not bother me, but it does. That is the truth. How am I supposed to stand up against my own relatives who blame me for what happened? I was not interested in him. He made me uncomfortable. I rejected his proposal kindly. I wanted to study further, I told him. He left in a huff and two days later, threw acid on my face. For what? To boost his ego? To make me suffer?' Her voice wavered with emotion. It seemed she would burst into tears any moment.

A spark ignited in Kannan's eyes. He rose to his feet, his every move emitting purpose. 'Pragya, you remind me of someone. Someone who lived years ago. One who changed the world,' he said.

Pragya stared at him, disbelieving. She perceived herself as someone who was powerless. How could she remind him of someone who had changed the world when she couldn't even save herself? she thought.

Without a pause, Kannan started to recite a verse from the Bhagavad Gita:

> *vepathuś cha śharīre me roma-harṣhaśh cha jāyate*
> *gāṇḍīvaṁ sraṁsate hastāt tvak chaiva paridahyate*
> *na cha śhaknomy avasthātuṁ bhramatīva cha me manaḥ*
> *nimittāni cha paśhyāmi viparītāni keśhava*
> *na cha śhreyo 'nupaśhyāmi hatvā sva-janam āhave'*

Chapter 1, Verses 29–31

I shiver, every hair on my skin standing on end. My bow feels heavy, slipping from my sweaty hands. I burn, but inside more than out. My mind spins, confused and scared. I can't even stand straight anymore. Krishna, you killed the Keshi demon, but all I see is bad happening. I don't understand how fighting my own family can be good.

'Do you know who said this?' he enquired.

'Yes, Arjuna said this to Krishna in the Shree Bhagavad Gita. My grandma would keep me close whenever she read it. It was my storybook growing up,' Pragya answered.

'Right. Arjuna too did not want to fight with his own kin, his own family. I am not here today to check how you are feeling. I am here today to see if you are ready,' he said.

'Ready for what?' she asked innocently.

'To see yourself through Arjuna's eyes. To accept that what happened wasn't your fault,' he stopped.

Pragya was an acid-attack survivor, the victim of a heinous crime committed about three years ago. Since then she had been battling, first to recover from physical injuries and medical complications and then to heal from the psychological trauma, social stigma and the daunting struggle of rebuilding her life—through visits to the court that forced her to relive the ordeal all over again. The process was emotionally draining, touching every aspect of her existence, whether it was justifying her feelings—to herself and to her family, questioning what she could have done differently, or even the silent agony of watching her parents suffer.

'I am not ready,' she said, her voice tinged with defeat. 'I am just not ready, Kannan. I am tired of explaining to everyone—my family, the lawyers, even the psychologists—that I am just exhausted. Just leave me alone.'

'You know, Pragya, when Arjuna found himself in a similar predicament, faced with a difficult choice—to fight and shed the blood of his own family or to abandon his duty as a Kshatriya warrior—he too, momentarily overwhelmed by the weight of this decision, put aside his bow and arrow and sat down in despair. There is no shame in feeling defeated.'

Tears welled up in Pragya's eyes. 'I am not ready to believe that this is all there is. I cannot accept that I will have to live with this version of my life forever,' she whispered.

Kannan continued, 'Accepting reality is not easy, I agree. We are all humans with a general tendency to resist what is uncomfortable, painful or inconvenient. You are not wrong when you feel uncomfortable about accepting your new reality.'

'Even if I accept, will others accept it?' she burst out.

'Does it matter?' he enquired.

'Yes, it does. They remind me of the incident every single day,' she said dismissively before sinking back into her chair.

'It would, if you keep looking at yourself through their eyes. But if you see yourself as who you are, then you will see a different picture,' Kannan said and sat down too, allowing his words to sink in.

Pragya finally looked up.

'It's human to want to shape our environment and our lives to our desires. To live the life we all imagined for ourselves. To please everyone. Yet, the harder we try to manipulate reality, the more we suffer. The more we cling to our expectations and ideals, the more we feel let down by life. The harder we grip the rope, the more the friction hurts us,' he continued thoughtfully.

'I agree, but it's not easy,' she said, realizing that it was the first time she had agreed with any of the counsellors.

'Then how can we break free from this cycle? How can we learn to accept what is, without giving up on our dreams and aspirations?' he asked.

'Dreams? I have no dreams anymore. And that is my reality now,' she said bitterly.

'Well, don't you dream that your family could go back to how it was? Don't you wish people looked at you like they used to? Those are dreams, Pragya. How can you say you don't have any?' Kannan asked, looking genuinely intrigued.

She sighed. There was no outsmarting this psychologist. Kannan was different, unlike the others before him. Therapists had dissected her words, offered textbook solutions, or tried too hard to fix her. Kannan did not try to impose his thinking on her. He listened. She felt safe with him. She felt she could talk to him endlessly, without pretence or the fear of being judged. He treated her like a person. With him, she felt normal.

'Yes, I have dreams. I want to get a job, go out with friends, live normally, get married, have children. I am only twenty-three after all,' she said, feeling some hope stirring within her.

Chintan: The Mirror

Kannan saw the sparkle in her eyes and smiled.

'I am glad you have finally acknowledged your dreams. The answer lies in radical acceptance, the practice of acknowledging and embracing reality as it is, without judgement, resistance or avoidance.

'What happened to you was unfair. So I want you to begin by writing down how you feel about this situation.' He handed Pragya a notepad with a pencil.

She started writing and within a minute filled the entire paper with raw unfiltered emotion. The words on the paper looked something like this:

> Why me! WHY? WHY DID IT HAVE TO HAPPEN TO ME. This is so unfair!
>
> I did not do anything wrong, then why do I have to go through this. It is so painful, everyday every part of my body hurts so much that I am unable to make out which part is hurting the most.
>
> I feel like killing myself so that I can just get over this pain once and for all. Not the physical pain, but the one I go through mentally every day!
>
> WHYYYY!!!!
>
> I feel so helpless right now, that even my tears have dried. I don't know what to feel and how to keep going. My mind goes blank when I try to think of the future.

She handed the paper back to Kannan. He looked at the paper and asked her, 'Now tell me, what is hurting the most right now?'

'I don't have a life anymore. My family has grown distant.

I have no friends and most of my time is spent nursing the wounds—the pain, tingling or burning sensation—that still exist due to the nerve damage. I feel like my body might never heal,' she explained.

'Okay, do you feel that your emotions have contributed to your suffering?' he questioned.

'No, he made me suffer. He is the reason why I am in this impossible situation,' she shouted.

'I understand but my question still remains. Do you think your *reactions* to your emotions have made you suffer?' he asked again.

She paused, taken aback.

He continued his enquiry. 'Have you ever found yourself lashing out at your family when the pain becomes overwhelming? Or have you given excuses to hide in your room when relatives visit?'

Pragya remained silent.

'Radical acceptance is neither about surrendering nor about accepting defeat. It is not even about giving up on yourself or your goals either. Rather, radical acceptance is about facing the truth of your situation and responding with clarity and compassion. Instead of clinging to a painful past, radical acceptance teaches us that letting go is essential to move beyond suffering. This doesn't mean suppressing emotions—it means allowing yourself to fully experience them and the pain but without letting those feelings evolve into prolonged suffering.

'When we stop resisting our reality, we cease fighting against ourselves and the world. We stop wasting our energy on blaming, resentment or regrets. We let go of the what-ifs.

Instead, we shift our focus on what is within our control—our thoughts, our actions, our attitude, our outlook and our response. We then begin to see new possibilities and opportunities that we might have previously missed. We start connecting with ourselves and others in a deeper, more authentic way,' Kannan explained.

'You mean that I have been so preoccupied struggling to accept what happened to me, how my life changed, that I never stopped to question whether some of that suffering was coming from me? Perhaps I was trapped in my own suffering because I was so consumed blaming him; I still do, because I am yet to make peace with what happened—why did he have to ruin my future? And honestly, I am not sure I ever truly will, even after today,' she admitted, while gazing outside the window.

'Yes, that is what I am trying to imply,' Kannan said, closely monitoring what Pragya might say next.

'I never thought of it that way,' she said in a hushed voice. Yet, she felt a sense of clarity that she hadn't experienced in a long time. She wanted to embrace the moment, however fleeting.

'It's okay. Radical acceptance, or acceptance for that matter, is not a one-time event. It's a lifelong practice that demands patience, courage and self-awareness. It's not easy letting go of our illusions, expectations and attachments. Or confronting our fears, doubts and insecurities,' Kannan clarified.

'I understand the essence of what you are saying. I have had some realizations during our conversation that I am eager to put into practice by taking some steps. Yet there is still one question you need to answer,' she demanded.

Kannan nodded.

'What about my face?' she asked, her voice breaking slightly. 'That's the first thing people see and no matter how much I work on my thoughts or my reactions, they will always see me like this. How do I come to terms with it?' she exclaimed.

dehino 'smin yathā dehe kaumāraṁ yauvanaṁ jarā
tathā dehāntara-prāptir dhīras tatra na muhyati

Chapter 2, Verse 12

The soul is eternal. Like the body passes from childhood to adulthood to old age until death, the soul too shall pass to another body. The wise are not deluded by this.

Pragya kept looking at Kannan.

Kannan continued:

na jāyate mriyate vā kadāchin
nāyaṁ bhūtvā bhavitā vā na bhūyaḥ
ajo nityaḥ śāśhvato 'yaṁ purāṇo
na hanyate hanyamāne śharīre

Chapter 2, Verse 20

The soul is neither born, nor does it ever die; nor having once existed, does it ever cease to be. The soul is without birth, eternal, immortal and ageless. It is not destroyed when the body is destroyed.

Kannan's words hit Pragya like a punch to the gut. She realized what he was trying to say.

He continued, 'Look beyond the mirror. See yourself

through the eyes of your soul. You will find beauty untouched by scars, and power that you hold beneath the surface. This body—this vessel—is temporary. What endures is your legacy—the memories you etch in the minds of others. Your courage in the courtroom for instance and its impact on other survivors.'

'Maybe you are right,' Pragya murmured, as if lost in deep thought.

Suddenly, sounds of broken glass thundered through the house followed by a loud thud that interrupted their conversation.

A red brick, heavy with dust and age, that had come sailing through the window, shattering its glass, now lay in the middle of the living room, a mute reminder of what Pragya's life had become. She had become a target to be mocked and teased by the neighbourhood children who regularly invented new ways to trouble her.

Alarm pulsed through Kannan. In near panic, he bolted across the room to the broken window to check who had thrown the brick at the window. 'Hey, who did this? Are you out of your mind? Someone could have gotten hurt!' he exclaimed, realizing the ordeal Pragya faced every day.

Pragya, however, remained rooted to her spot, lost in thought, calm in a storm she had grown used to surviving. Her mind unravelled memories like old film reels, one frame at a time. She wasn't shocked by the sudden intrusion. She understood what she had endured. Like a mantra, she repeated to herself,

> *'Far enough I have come*
> *Far enough I have to go'*

Without warning she walked to the door and headed outside. Kannan wordlessly followed her with a knowing smile—it was quite unexpected but long overdue. He stayed a few paces behind her, giving her space, yet offering silent strength.

She descended the stairs and made her way past the threshold. She exited the main entrance. Her mother came running behind her and shouted, 'Pragya, where are you going? Come back, *beta*.'

Kannan politely signalled reassurance, gesturing to her that he would remain with Pragya.

Meanwhile, Pragya stood outside her house, in the chaos and noise of a busy street, her eyes scanning the spectators, trying to fathom their thoughts. They had been counting on her vulnerability for too long. But not anymore, she thought determinedly to herself.

Usually she was afraid of what they might say or, worse, throw at her, but today power coursed through her. She faced the people who had witnessed her growth from a young girl to a young woman. They knew her well. Yet they felt like strangers now.

The neighbourhood aunty whom Pragya had nursed through pneumonia—when she was confined to bed and even her own children hadn't shown up; the sweet *Chacha*, who she used to greet with smiles every day while going to college; the young boy who lived in a house on the adjacent street, whom she had tutored to clear middle school; the beggar for whom she had sneaked out dinner so often; and all the others who had been part of her small, kind world. Before the acid attack.

Pragya was like a bright ray of sunshine, compassionate

and loving with everyone who had known her. Yet so much had changed almost overnight. These same people had earlier praised her for the way she looked, even called her beautiful and suggested suitable boys for her marriage. After the acid attack, she had become a freak show for these people who were unable to see her beyond her disfigurement. She had significantly lost the vision in her left eye and most of the skin on her face had melted like a burning candle.

Yet for the first time in three painful years, Pragya had stepped out of the house without the scarf that had guarded her face like an armour. The once-revered piece of clothing now lay inconsequential somewhere in her room. It was no longer needed. Without it, her face was on full display.

The crowd gaped at her with raw emotion: disgust, shock, pity, even contempt.

Pragya stood tall amid the hostile crowd, meeting every gaze—even the children, whose laughter faded in the face of her quiet strength. She stood bold, unapologetic and unmoved. Her eyes reflected her courage and pride, burning with something more fierce and powerful—acceptance of herself. And also the questions that still remained.

For once, she did not question her sanctity or her own individuality, but of those staring at her.

'What did I do to deserve the bricks being hurled at me? Why do you treat me as if I have committed a crime? When did my scars become more offensive than the act that caused them?' she thundered. 'When did my face overpower the kindness I once showered on you?'

The crowd remained silent. Most eyes looked down at the ground as if in shame. When someone is a victim of an acid attack, it is not only the face and body that burns. The acid burns through dreams, self-esteem, strength, and upturns an entire life. It's not just the skin it scars, it sears into the victim's sanity. It is not only the survivor who undergoes severe trauma, it is an entire family. An acid attack is not just tragic, it's monstrous. It's a coward's way of extinguishing the fire of ego and rejection.

For the past three years, Pragya had carried the weight of shame and embarrassment. But not today. No more.

Every person she stared back at had their eyes down in shame. Shame for treating her differently, for making her feel alienated and rejected, for the stones thrown into her home, for the dismembered relationships and lack of fellowship, and for making it tougher on her than it already was. Here and now, she reclaimed a piece of herself.

So what was different today? What changed?

Pragya had changed. She was finally free.

3

Vivek: Truth vs Illusion

'Stop, stop, *bhaiya*. Open the door,' she shouted frantically, pounding on the door. But he wouldn't listen. She kept calling out to her parents, 'Mom, dad, please call someone. Break open this door.' Yet, no one was coming to her aid.

The pounding on the door kept getting louder and louder and suddenly with a jerk, Raya woke up. It was a dream. Her face was wet with tears. She was drenched in sweat.

Breathing heavily, she recognized that it was the same nightmare she had been having for the past seven years. Waking up like this was a familiar feeling.

Time had passed, but the echoes of that day still rang loud in her mind—the cries of 'Stop!', the pounding on the door, the chaos, the commotion, and ultimately the shock and the heavy silence of loss that lingered. It felt like it had happened just yesterday.

Her past clung to her like a shadow, full of unanswered questions and the ache of separation.

Shaking her head to push away these thoughts, she rose

from the bed in her hotel, still somewhat distracted, to ease into her day.

She dressed in her usual attire; a chikankari kurta with a pair of blue denim jeans and some silver *jhumka*s. She reminded herself of the long day ahead at work. She had deadlines to chase and she couldn't afford to lose focus.

She stepped out the door to head to work, unaware that fate was going to work a twist in today's routine. Her past was going to collide with her present—uninvited yet unstoppable. The answers she had yearned for, for years, might finally come today.

She reached the popular street where a row of cafés and casual eateries served up a vibrant mix of flavours. 'Sir, what do you think about the quality of the food available here?' she asked a random man on the street.

She was a features writer with a local newspaper. She'd recently been handed what felt like the dullest assignment yet—going through the streets of the city to collect public opinion on food. Not convinced about this mission, she suspected that she had been chosen as she was a self-declared foodie. Today's stop was a bustling food street in Delhi.

She spent the entire morning weaving through crowds of people, questioning them under the sweltering sun. The heat clung to her skin and her throat felt parched. It was afternoon by the time she quickly ducked into a café for a much-needed break—and food.

The café's cool comfort and the familiar aroma of South Indian food took her back to her mother's kitchen. The café served simple, traditional food on a banana leaf with flavours that mirrored the taste of her mother's recipes. It was one of her favourite restaurants in the city.

The meals here reminded her of the warmth of her Amma's food and healing hugs. She remembered how Amma would hug her when she returned home and place before her a plate of her fragrant rasam and rice. That was all it took to make her feel better on the worst days. This café was a non-negotiable as she was heading out to Aurangabad tomorrow.

She looked around for an empty table, but the café seemed to be full. She was starving and the fragrance of aromatic spices was not helping either. Hunger gnawed at her being. She waited, hoping one of the tables would clear up.

Just then, a waiter approached and asked, 'Do you mind sharing a table? There's only one spot or you could wait about 15 minutes.'

Grateful for this opportunity, she nodded and replied, 'I don't mind sharing a table. Please lead me to it.'

Raya followed the waiter who led her through the bustling café to the table and quickly headed back to the kitchen. She, however, remained rooted to her spot, her breath caught in her throat. Shock washed over her. She couldn't believe what she was seeing.

Could it be? It has to be her, she battled with her thoughts, her heart refusing to believe what her eyes saw. Seated at the table was a face she hadn't seen in years. The woman Raya was about to share the table with was Aanyahi.

Aanyahi and Raya's story traced back to the corridors of college. Aanyahi had been the introvert, shy and sober, while Raya was the bubbly extrovert who had welcomed Aanyahi into her world and quickly introduced her to her wide circle of friends.

Within a few months, Raya and Aanyahi were always together. From attending classes to celebrating college fests, even helping Amma in the kitchen. They were inseparable.

Aanyahi had become almost a second daughter to Raya's parents, adorably blurring the line between friends and family—especially after she started dating Raya's elder brother, Rohan.

Everything seemed picture perfect, until one day everything unravelled.

Seven years had passed since they had parted ways. Abruptly. But like the people who remain warm in our memory, deeply etched in our mind, heart and life, Aanyahi wasn't forgotten—for reasons both good and bad. And in all honesty, Raya had never truly moved on.

Caught off guard, Raya stood perplexed, unsure how to navigate this unexpected reunion. For a moment, she was tempted by an inexplicable urge to quickly turn around and leave, yet she sensed that all the answers she needed were finally within reach—if she dared to take the chance.

Am I even ready to face her? What would I say? More so, will she even want to talk? Raya thought. It wasn't just the fear of confrontation; it was perhaps the fear of abandonment or losing a dear friend once again.

Raya stoically walked to the table and settled in a chair across from Aanyahi. Beside her sat a man—somewhat older yet intriguing in appearance. He exuded an effortless charisma that was mesmerizing.

The waiter immediately handed Raya a menu with a smile as she sat down, before attending to another customer. Raya gently placed the menu on the table and looked directly at Aanyahi. As their eyes met, the shock in Aanyahi's expression was unmistakable. Meeting here in a crowded café was unexpected, almost impossible.

'Raya?' Aanyahi whispered, her eyes wide, clearly finding herself at a loss for words.

'Hi, Aanyahi. What an absolute surprise! I haven't seen you in seven years!' Raya's voice also betrayed a nervous squeak.

Raya took Aanyahi's hand in hers and gave it a gentle squeeze.

'Umm, this is my friend, Kannan,' Aanyahi said, recovering. We both happened to be in the city today, so we had to meet. A lot of coincidences are happening today,' she added with a light laugh.

'You both know each other?' Kannan asked, sensing a strange tension in the air.

'Yes, we were college friends. Long ago,' Raya responded. Kannan nodded, tapping into some awkwardness between these two women—a mixture of guilt and confusion or pain that demanded closure. Raya seemed anxious, while Aanyahi looked as if she had been waiting for this reunion to happen.

Today, she would finally have the chance to share her side of the story.

Aanyahi was about to say something when the waiter stepped to their table to take their order. Aanyahi ordered her favourite, masala dosa.[2] Raya chuckled and ordered the same for herself with filter coffee. Kannan ordered a plate

---

[2] Masala dosa is a thin, crispy crepe (dosa) filled with a spiced potato filling (masala).

of idli sambhar.[3] As the waiter left, Aanyahi said, 'This is my favourite café!'

'Mine too,' Raya grinned in excitement.

'It reminds me of Amma,' they both said in unison, sounding as if it was rehearsed. They shared a surprised laugh.

After a pause, Raya spoke, 'You left without a word. I mean, I did not get it. I needed you the most then. Why? I know we have just met after seven years; we have company and this may not be the best time; but I have to know why you left.'

'I withdrew from college, Raya,' Aanyahi confessed, her voice filled with a blend of vulnerability and resilience.

'I just had to leave. I had no choice,' she continued, looking down as she fidgeted with the napkin in front of her, trying to mask her guilt.

Kannan just sat there listening to the conversation.

'You had no choice? What does that even mean?' Raya's tone sharpened, her temper rising. 'Do you know what I have been through? I've spent years reliving our past, Aanyahi. It haunts me even now and I still don't know the why,' she confessed, her voice quivering.

'I was just a kid back then, Raya. I was hurting too,' Aanyahi shot back.

'I lost my brother! And I lost my best friend,' Raya said, as her voice cracked. She couldn't control her tears.

'Hey, both of you take a breath please. Calm down. First,

---

[3]Idli sambhar is a popular South Indian dish where soft, steamed cakes made of fermented rice and lentils, called idli, are served with a flavourful lentil and vegetable stew called sambhar.

I don't know what this conversation is about, but clearly it is important to both of you. So just take a moment,' Kannan said in a soothing voice.

Silence followed. After a while, Raya spoke.

'After Rohan died by suicide, I was mad at you. I blamed you for it. I believed you were the cause of his suffering, that you ruined our lives. A part of me still does. Amma went into depression. Baba couldn't stop blaming himself. Rohan's death and your disappearance took away all the happiness we had known. It took us years to get on with our lives.'

'Raya,' Aanyahi replied, her voice steady but laced with sadness. 'I too carried a burden of guilt for what happened to Rohan and what happened between us. I believed I had brought nothing but tragedy into your lives. I blamed myself for the pain your family had to endure. I couldn't bear to see that, so I transferred colleges to Bangalore. But you need to understand that I too lost someone I loved. It all happened in front of my eyes. It still haunts me.'

'What?' Raya's eyes widened.

'Look at me, Aanyahi. What did you just say?'

Aanyahi looked up, tears flowing down her face. 'Yes, I was on a video call with him when he did it.'

Aanyahi's words sent a chill down Raya's spine. Time and space ceased to matter. Both Raya and Kannan could not believe what they had just heard. Raya just stared at Aanyahi, numb. All these years, she'd painted herself as the victim. She had no idea about the horror of what Aanyahi had witnessed or its impact on her.

'You never told me, Aanyahi,' Kannan said, shaken by

what Aanyahi had endured and for having missed the reason for the sadness in her eyes.

'Rohan struggled with depression. He was in therapy. Your father knew, which is probably why he blames himself. I tried helping Rohan. I loved him so much. But his anxiety often got the better of him. He was always afraid. Afraid that he would not be able to do well in life. Or he would lose his loved ones. He lived more in a speculated negative future than in the present. That day I had to visit my aunt who was in the last stage of cancer and really suffering. Rohan called me and I tried to help him too, but it all escalated so quickly. And then he did it, in front of my eyes. He just kept the phone on the table facing himself so that I could see all of it. I saw him stand up on the chair and, and.... I just kept shouting his name; I kept telling him to stop, begged him not to do this to me. I also kept calling your dad from my aunt's phone. I don't know—I have never felt so helpless,' Aanyahi was in tears. She was sobbing. 'I kept shouting his name...until I fainted. By the time I recovered, it was all over. He was gone. Just like that.'

'I am so sorry, Aanyahi. I never knew all this. Why didn't you tell me? Why didn't you return?' Raya said, feeling disgusted with herself for having thought the worst of Aanyahi all these years.

'I couldn't face you. Or Amma. I had failed Rohan. I had lost him. Naturally everyone blamed me. I did too. So I just had to get away,' Aanyahi said, holding Raya's hand. They sat in silence, the years between them just melting away with understanding and forgiveness.

Vivek: Truth vs Illusion • 49

Finally Kannan spoke. 'None of you is to blame. I hope you understand that after all these years.' Aanyahi knew what was coming.

Kannan quoted from the Bhagavad Gita.

indriyāṇi mano buddhir asyādhiṣhṭhānam uchyate
etair vimohayatyeṣha jñānam āvṛitya dehinam
tasmāt tvam indriyāṇyādau niyamya bharatarṣhabha
pāpmānaṁ prajahi hyenaṁ jñāna-vijñāna-nāśhanam

Chapter 3, Verse 40-41

Our senses, mind and intellect are like fertile ground where desires are sown. These desires, when unchecked, can cloud our wisdom and mislead our true self, the embodied soul. Therefore, Arjuna, the best of the Bharatas, the first step is to conquer these desires and vanquish this internal enemy that embodies sin and destroys both knowledge and self-realization.

Raya shot a questioning gaze at Aanyahi, who politely nodded while wiping her tears. 'He is getting to a point. Listen,' she said as Kannan continued.

'This verse speaks about how desire governs our lives by using our senses, mind and intellect as its instruments. It often clouds our judgement, distorting reason and leading us to act against our better nature. In its grip, we lose clarity—and from that confusion, ignorance arises. Rohan acted out of ignorance. He did not know what he was doing. He was incapable of considering the consequences of his choices or its impact on those he loved.'

Both Aanyahi and Raya nodded in unison, holding each

other to share the pain they both had endured for seven long years.

Aanyahi said thoughtfully, 'I was being ignorant too, driven by the desire to survive. When I saw everyone I knew turning against me and blaming me, I was filled with fear. I assumed they would not believe me. So I took flight instead of even trying to bring out the truth.'

'Yes, your will to survive outweighed your need to reason,' Kannan replied.

'What about me?' Raya asked quietly.

Before Kannan could reply, the food arrived and as the waiter placed the plates of food before them, they inhaled the aroma which was therapeutic by itself. When the waiter left, Kannan continued.

'You, my friend, were also driven by ignorance, like your brother, oblivious and unaware about the situation, perhaps unknowingly. Yet part of you stayed tethered to what had happened instead of trying to find your friend to see how she was coping,' Kannan said.

A storm stirred within Raya. 'You know, Kannan, in the whirlwind of our daily lives, we get so caught up in the chaos that we often overlook the struggles of others or remain unaware that they too are silently struggling. We forget to empathize or understand their pain. Like I did with Aanyahi. I was too absorbed in my own sorrow to even try to understand her part or what she had been through. I was so oblivious to her loss that I made myself the only victim. I kept blaming her instead. In this situation, forgiveness felt impossible. We victimize ourselves because that is easy,' Raya said.

'It wasn't just on you, Raya. Had I just told the truth

instead of running away, maybe everything would have turned out differently,' Aanyahi countered softly.

Kannan leaned back, his eyes distant. He then said, 'This reminds me of another shloka from the Gita.'

*dhūmenāvriyate vahnir yathādarśo malena cha
yatholbenāvṛito garbhas tathā tenedam āvṛitam*

Chapter 3, Verse 38

Just as smoke obscures fire, dust hides a mirror, and the womb shelters an embryo, so too can uncontrolled desire cloud our knowledge.

'Look at both of you. Action is the essence of life, but its quality or worth hinges *not* on the act itself, but on its driving forces.

'When Krishna urges Arjuna to embrace *niyatam karma*—actions performed with a sense of duty and without attachment to the outcome or expectation of personal gain, he also warns him against *kamya karma*, actions fuelled by desire, and *nishiddha karma*, which are acts that blatantly violate one's moral code.

'Aanyahi, your duty was to reveal the truth without fear of its consequences. Raya, your duty was to seek the truth rather than being clouded by your judgement of the situation. Rohan too fell into the trap of *nishiddha karma*. His desires had taken over his mind and blinded him from being able to differentiate between right and wrong, or what was ethical or unethical.

'Everyone caught in the aftermath of Rohan's actions repeated the pattern—seeking either revenge or refuge. No one paused to find the truth until now. Raya, as Rohan's sister, you channelled your pain to blame Aanyahi for your suffering. You wanted Aanyahi too to suffer. This desire kept you from finding out what really happened. And you, Aanyahi, were so consumed with your desire to seek refuge away from the chaos and blame, that you never tried to set the truth free.'

'Then how do we break free from this cycle, this pattern?' Raya asked.

'First, you must let go of the different biases that cloud your thinking. There are six biases. Have you heard of them? Confirmation bias, conviction bias, appearance bias, the group bias, blame bias and superiority bias,' Kannan asked.

'And how do these work?' Aanyahi asked.

'With **confirmation** bias we "find" or interpret new information or evidence as confirmation of an existing belief or theory that only makes the belief stronger. Under **conviction** bias we defend an idea we want to believe rather than being open to nuances. We look for evidence to convince ourselves that what we believe is true. With an **appearance** bias, we judge others on the basis of how they look. The **group** bias promotes a herd mentality or it occurs when we provide preferential treatment to others in the same group. The **blame** bias pushes us to blame others or even circumstances for our failure rather than accepting responsibility for our actions. The **superiority** bias influences us to overestimate our own qualities or abilities and underrate others. These biases have the power to influence how we perceive and weigh information, leading to skewed judgements and decisions,' he explained, before asking, 'Which bias clouded your judgement in this situation, Raya?'

'Confirmation and blame bias. I took the situation at face

value and squarely blamed Aanyahi for it,' Raya admitted.

'Good, acceptance is the key to moving on,' Kannan said and continued.

'To think rationally in a situation, one must question everything. To do this requires scepticism,' he concluded.

'How can one think rationally when there is so much going on?' Aanyahi asked.

'It's certainly not easy, but by cultivating one simple habit, you can,' Kannan said.

'What is that?' Raya asked.

'Take some time to respond. Pause before you react.'

'In intense moments as a situation is unfolding, our thoughts are naturally scattered. To provide direction to these chaotic thoughts, we must allow ourselves the space and take some time to reflect or to seek guidance before we can make sense of what is happening to make a decision or respond.'

'It is easier said than done,' exclaimed Aanyahi.

'Really? Let me share with you a story. I read it in the book *Stillness is the Key* by the author Ryan Holiday,' Kannan elaborated.

'In 1962 during the Cuban Missile Crisis, the world stood on the brink of a nuclear war. American deployments of nuclear missiles in Italy and Turkey were matched by Soviet deployments of nuclear missiles in Cuba. At the time, J.F. Kennedy was the president of the United States and Nikita Khrushchev was the Soviet First Secretary.

'Earlier at the Vienna summit, sensing Kennedy's political weakness, Khrushchev had repeatedly denied the presence of any Soviet weapons in Cuba. Subsequently, when Soviet missiles were discovered, Kennedy was advised to let American troops invade Cuba. America believed invasion of Cuba was the only solution. But Kennedy remained calm. He reflected for days. Then he chose patience over provocation. He demanded the withdrawal of missiles from Cuba instead of launching a war. He imposed a naval quarantine, carefully avoiding the term "blockade", which by legal definition meant "an act of war", to prevent the situation from escalating.

'By staying calm, Kennedy demonstrated that it is possible to avoid the negative implications of impulsive actions when we think through situations. We need to give ourselves time to heal, to let go of anger before rushing into decisions that we are bound to regret. When someone lashes out or behaves negatively—be it a colleague's angry outburst, a friend suddenly withdrawing contact, or even a loved one becoming distant—our instinct is often to confront them. Instead, we can demonstrate some empathy, which is a more powerful response. It means to take a moment for reflection, to pause before reacting; listening to truly understand or even trying to perceive a situation through the other's perspective. Imagine responding to someone's distress not with judgement, but with curiosity about their inner struggles. This is empathy in action—a conscious choice to connect with another, to acknowledge their hardship and offer support when most needed,' Kannan paused. Looking at Raya and Aanyahi, he narrated another verse from the Bhagavad Gita.

ātmaupamyena sarvatra samaṁ paśhyati yo 'rjuna
sukhaṁ vā yadi vā duḥkhaṁ sa yogī paramo mataḥ

Chapter 6, Verse 32

He is a perfect yogi who, by comparison to his own self, sees the true equality of all beings, in both their happiness and their distress, O Arjuna.

'Here the lord tells Arjuna that the one who sees all individuals as equal to himself and practises true empathy by living his joy or sorrow as if they are his own is a true yogi. He goes beyond mere sympathy; he practises a state of consciousness where the boundaries between self and others diminish,' Kannan explained.

We all are one. One Universe.

4
Mukti: Breaking Free

Aakash rose from his slumber with the gentle glow of the rising sun touching his face, already wearied by the weight of exhaustion before the day had even begun. Sleep never seemed to rest Aakash, for he could almost never get enough of it.

Each day he woke up on the hard floor, sharply aware of how his day ahead would unfold—cycling for hours to deliver food in his vicinity for customers who had ordered through an online food-ordering app. His days looped like clockwork; wake, ride, deliver, repeat. Often, he felt he wasn't really living but merely surviving. What hurt him the most was how his daily earnings were ironically lower than the price of the food he ferried to his customers. I am just another cog in this city, he thought to himself.

Suddenly his phone pinged to life. Bleary-eyed, he saw an order on the food-delivery app. It must have been 5 a.m. in the morning. 'Seriously? Who even orders this early? Don't people have kitchens?' he grumbled to himself.

Aakash got up, still grumpy as he wore the company

uniform and prepared for the day. Heading out, he looked at his bicycle. The same bike he once loved to ride carefree like the wind, it mocked him now. It reminded him of his tireless responsibilities. I should be joyfully chasing cricket balls with my friends, not food orders for unknown customers, he thought. He cursed under his breath. He had to let go of his studies to work as a food-delivery agent to earn for his family after his father was paralysed a year ago. Since then he had been doing odd jobs to make a living.

Shrugging away the thought, he clipped his phone to the handlebar of his cycle and started out to pick up the first order of the day. While he was on his way to deliver someone's breakfast, he realized that he hadn't had any himself.

His legs started to pedal as the city stirred to life around him; shops opening their doors, newspaper boys going through the streets, and birds chirping in the morning air.

He was forced to choose a bicycle over a motorbike due to financial and age constraints, but it limited his capacity for making deliveries as he could only get orders within a five-kilometre radius of his chosen centre. Although he had learned to optimize time and make more deliveries to compensate for his lack of speed, the rewards were never enough to make ends meet.

Today's first delivery was three kilometres out from the restaurant. He scanned his phone to check for traffic and mapped the fastest route through the city.

Being a daydreamer, he dreamt of a better life while cycling. He didn't know how or when but he knew one day he would do well—when money would be abundant and he would not have to toil for hours to earn a meagre amount or struggle to make ends meet. He could visualize himself driving a car of his own. He dreamt of owning a shiny new pair of leather shoes.

While he was busy in his thoughts, riding mindlessly, he didn't see the car until it was too late. Tyres screeched as the car braked and the driver swerved away from the cyclist. Aakash also tried to apply the brakes but as the bicycle skidded wildly, only a single thought occurred in this mind—the food! Instinctively, he threw himself sideways, abandoning his own safety to protect the delivery bag in his arms. As he fell to the ground, throbbing pain radiated out from his twisted ankle. However, the order remained safe. The car driver sped away.

◆

Slumped by the side of the road, clutching his painful ankle with both his hands, Aakash's thoughts spiralled. I am going to be late. How can I deliver this order? I will not be paid for this delivery otherwise. Why does this keep happening to me? I need to get up somehow. 'Get up, Aakash,' he commanded himself.

He groaned and forced himself to sit up but tentative attempts to rise intensified his pain. However, his eyes held the steely glint of resolve. Every minute wasted meant less money. He had bills to pay and a target to reach. He had to keep going.

Mustering all his strength, he somehow managed to stand without putting pressure on his ankle and mount his bike, but seconds later found himself sprawled on the ground once again. He couldn't get up. Jolts of pain shot up through his injured leg. His ankle hurt so much that he could barely walk; pedalling was out of the question.

Defeated, he sat back down on the pavement, crying. All he could think about was the money he would lose and the inevitable reprimand from the app's customer service team. They wouldn't understand that this is not my fault, he thought to himself helplessly in between sobs.

Suddenly out of nowhere, a stranger stood before Aakash, extending a helping hand.

'Hey, are you alright? That was quite a nasty fall,' the stranger asked in a voice exuding genuine concern.

Aakash blinked, startled. No one else had even looked his way or cared enough to help him up, let alone ask if he was okay.

Aakash noticed that the stranger had long hair and a kind face that was lit up by a smile. His face was as calm as the moon, his eyes shining like sapphires. It was Kannan, somehow, always showing up in the right place at the right time.

Aakash wasn't used to kindness. Life hadn't offered him much. With some hesitation and quiet disbelief, Aakash stretched out his hand and accepted Kannan's help. With a touch of scepticism, he said, 'Yeah, I had a little accident here.'

'Can you walk?' Kannan asked.

'Not exactly. My ankle hurts a lot and I am unable to pedal.'

'Why don't you rest a while?' Kannan suggested.

'I cannot. I need to deliver this order or I won't get paid,' Aakash said, tears welling up in his eyes. Life had forced him to grow up fast.

Since his father's paralysis a year ago, his mother had struggled to feed her five children. Aakash, as the oldest son, had felt compelled to take on the role of provider. He lied about his age and found a job with the food-delivery company. The hunger-stricken cries of his toddler siblings still haunted him. He had sworn to never let them sleep hungry. Yet he would have to return home without any money, knowing he could not pedal for at least a day more with all the pain, Aakash thought with a pang of guilt.

Kannan's calm face tightened with concern for the boy. He took the phone from Aakash's hand and called a number.

When the call was answered, Kannan started to speak, 'Hi there, I am Kannan. I am calling on behalf of Aakash. He has met with an accident and I am taking him to the hospital. I think his ankle is broken. Can you please send a delivery agent at Palam Vihar Chowk to deliver the order?'

'NO!' Aakash shouted. 'They will not pay me if I don't complete the delivery and I am almost there.'

'I'll pay you for this delivery, but you must come with me to the hospital. You need to see a doctor for this injury, okay?' Kannan said gently.

'I am Kannan, consider me your friend. I am just trying to help you as you do need to see a doctor. What is your name?' Kannan asked as he assisted Aakash up.

'I am Aakash, I live nearby.' By now, Aakash's tears had slowly turned into dry sobs arising entirely from the pain he was going through.

◆

At the hospital, an X-ray revealed a minor fracture in Aakash's ankle. As the doctor set the plaster, Aakash sat in silence. Kannan sat beside him, quietly observing Aakash's face clouded with sadness and sensing the storm of thoughts brewing within the young boy.

The doctor completed the task and left. He advised Aakash to leave the hospital a couple of hours after the plaster had stabilized, which would also provide time for deeper injuries, if any, to surface. The impact from the fall had been strong and Aakash needed to rest his leg over the next few weeks.

Kannan sat near the bed, facing Aakash. He smiled and said, 'You'll be fine now.'

'How can I be fine? I won't be able to earn for at least fifteen days. The doctor said it is a minor fracture, but I still need to rest. With this plaster on my leg, how will I even pedal? I can barely walk,' Aakash's words tumbled out in desperation, reflecting his state of panic at not being able to earn.

The stranger's eyes sparkled with wisdom as he spoke. 'Accidents sometimes uncover truths we don't want to face.'

Aakash shot Kannan a sceptical look and snapped, 'Truths? I don't need riddles. Life is tough enough as it is. Don't give me philosophy.'

Kannan could clearly sense that Aakash was experiencing multiple emotions simultaneously—anger, guilt, shame, irritation, fear and pain—under the drowsiness caused by the medicines. It was too much for the young boy to handle.

Kannan smiled serenely. 'Aakash, it is precisely when life is at its toughest that we must pause and reflect on the purpose of our actions.'

Aakash shook his head, frustration creeping into his voice. 'Purpose? I'm just trying to earn a living for my family to survive in this world. Do you think this accident is going to solve even a single one of my problems?' The boy was weary from the medications, so Kannan just let him sleep.

◆

'Listen carefully,' Kannan said after Aakash woke up and nursed a sandwich with a cup of tea. 'I will tell you a secret today. Lord Krishna in Chapter 4 *Jnana Yoga* of the Bhagavad Gita said:

*na māṁ karmāṇi limpanti na me karma-phale spṛihā
iti māṁ yo 'bhijānāti karmabhir na sa badhyate*

Chapter 4, Verse 14

'This means that by pursuing an action with the desire for personal gain, we find ourselves trapped in a cycle of karmic reactions. When we obsess over outcomes, we become entangled in the very consequences we seek to control, impacting our present and future potential. We must therefore focus on performing our duties without expecting anything in return or without attachment to results.'

Aakash listened intently. 'It is easy for you to say. I have a family to support. I cannot work without expecting money in return,' he replied hastily.

Aakash's life circumstances had prematurely aged him, making him bitter. Kannan felt a pang of sympathy for a moment but his determination to help the boy deepened.

Kannan's gaze softened. 'I understand your concerns, my

friend. But what if I told you that by performing your duties with dedication and the right attitude, you may find what you truly seek?' Kannan's voice conveyed gentle reassurance.

Aakash's impatience flared. 'Fulfilment? I need tangible results, not vague notions. I have bills to pay.' His scepticism seemed stronger.

Kannan's voice remained steady, a soothing balm to Aakash's restless mind. 'I hear you. Feeding your family, isn't that your duty?'

'Yes,' Aakash replied.

'And your duty also lies with the customers to whom you deliver the food?'

Aakash fell silent for a moment. He had never looked at it that way. 'I guess yes. But how do you define duty?' he asked.

Kannan's eyes gleamed. 'Ah, an interesting question. Duty primarily begins with responsibility towards immediate family, friends and society at large. Every mind determines those duties based on individual desires. Once the mind rises above these personal desires, then one is ready to begin the journey inward, toward discovering the self,' Kannan said.

'So, my friend, your duty is not just to feed your family, but also to serve others because every action done in the right spirit is a form of prayer,' Kannan continued.

'All that sounds noble but does not change the fact that I have a broken ankle. This idea will bring me out of neither poverty nor the situation in which I am stuck. I cannot deliver food for the next fifteen days. How do I rise above that?' Aakash enquired.

'By facing it!' Kannan replied firmly, with a jolt. 'You have a broken ankle and cannot cycle to deliver food. But you can study. Use this time well. Dig into your savings. You have savings, right?' Kannan enquired.

'Yes, a little,' said Aakash, disheartened. It was all that remained of what his father had left for the family and clearly would not last long.

Kannan pressed on. 'Then tell me something. You are fifteen, you bear the responsibility of supporting your family and you have limited savings. Do you believe delivering food will always be the best way to provide for your family?'

'If I can now, why not later?' Aakash asked.

'Aakash, you need to face your reality. Let me explain something.'

Kannan picked up some paper napkins from the table near Aakash's bed. He took out his pen and started drawing something on it. An idea that could change Aakash's perspective.

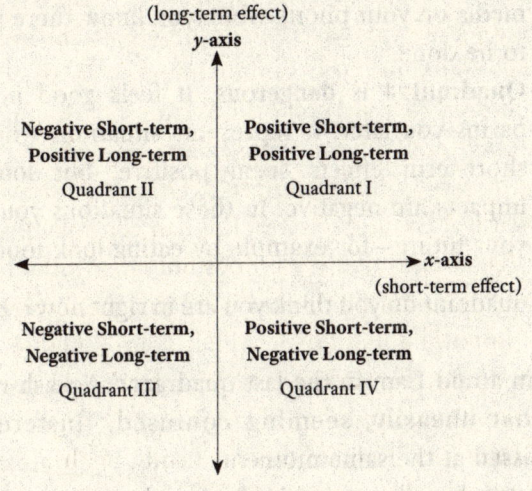

'Look here. This is a graph that represents long-term impacts on the y-axis and short-term effects on the x-axis. Life can be mapped on this graph,' Kannan said as he explained each quadrant.

- **'Quadrant 1** is the sweet spot, where both the short-term and long-term outcomes are positive. This quadrant represents the most ideal situation. For example, building good relationships.
- **Quadrant 2** is tough discipline now, rewards later. It represents negative short-term effects but positive long-term effects. In these situations, you are inconveniencing yourself. Sacrificing in the present for a better future. For example, going to bed on time.
- **Quadrant 3** represents poor choices. It is the worst, where both the short-term and long-term effects are negative. Think mindless scrolling through social media on your phone when you know there is work to be done.
- **Quadrant 4** is dangerous. It feels good now but harms you later. It represents situations where the short-term effects seem positive, but long-term impacts are negative. In these situations you wreck your future—for example by eating junk food.

'Which quadrant do you think you are in right now?' Kannan asked.

'I am afraid I am in the last quadrant?' Aakash replied, somewhat uneasily, seeming confused, flustered and embarrassed at the same moment.

'Yes, my friend, you are in the fourth quadrant. You are

somehow surviving in the present, but unable to focus on your future. There is no long-term plan.' Kannan paused, then asked Aakash, 'How do you think you can come out of it?'

Kannan believed that the answers to our questions lie within us. Had he simply provided Aakash the answer to this question, the boy might never have grasped its true depth. However, now that Aakash was quizzing himself for the answers, he would realize things with greater clarity. So Kannan waited.

Aakash answered slowly but surely. 'By building my future alongside my daily struggles. By shifting focus to my studies, perhaps I won't have to deliver food forever.' Aakash's response seemed to emanate from deep within, as if a realization had dawned on him. 'Exactly! You must strive to look at situations from a wider perspective. Unless you uplift yourself, how do you think you can uplift others? I am now certain there was a purpose to this accident. It happened to compel you to slow down and realize what needs to be done. Your duty to serve others continues, but now you can fulfil it with a clear intention. It is on you how to maximize it,' Kannan replied, his voice filled with contentment.

Aakash realized that he was driven by the necessity of survival and had approached his work with the familiar question, 'How will this benefit me?' He was solely seeking immediate, tangible results and focused on the practical aspects of his daily grind.

'I know what you are thinking. We all work to survive. But there is more than survival, there is living. You know Aakash, it has never been about surviving. We've got it all wrong,' Kannan said.

'I don't understand,' said Aakash confused.

'See, it has always been about living. It has always been about making a life. Survival is not the ultimate goal; it's a prerequisite for living, for creating, for evolving. We exist not merely to endure but to thrive, to contribute and to make a ripple. Hunting to survive was not the sole purpose of our ancestors; it was a way to sustain life and pursue their passions. Their existence was not about merely surviving but about making a difference, about shaping the world around them.

'The millions who pass away each day, whether due to old age, accidents or sheer bad luck, did not fail to survive; they fulfilled their purpose of living. They contributed to society, nurtured relationships and left behind a legacy, however small.

'Even death, in its inevitable cycle, serves a greater purpose. It makes way for new life, new beginnings, new opportunities to create and innovate. The world moves forward, not just because we survive but because we live, because we love, because we create. Do you follow?' asked Kannan.

'Yes,' said Aakash.

Kannan believed that Aakash would soon realize true fulfilment lay not in the destination alone, but in the journey itself. The purpose behind his actions would be revealed as he approached each day with dedication and the right attitude.

tasmād ajñāna-sambhūtaṁ hṛit-sthaṁ jñānāsinātmanaḥ
chhittvainaṁ sanśhayaṁ yogam ātiṣhṭhottiṣhṭha bhārata

Chapter 4, Verse 42

Therefore, having cut with the weapon of knowledge the doubts born of ignorance that lie in your heart, establish yourself in yoga, and arise, O Bharata.

Rise, and take actions!

Aakash closed his eyes and took a deep breath. The medicines and the food were again making him drowsy. Yet, he tried to cling to the clarity the conversation had sparked.

He wanted to register everything Kannan had said. It all made sense somehow. How he needed to mindfully shift his perspective about his situation by moving from the fourth quadrant to the second quadrant, the path of purpose. Wanting to continue the conversation, he managed to open his eyes but was shocked to see no one there. Kannan was gone. On his bedside was kept ₹500. Aakash just smiled as something stirred within him.

A realization dawned and a sense of wonder filled his heart. Perhaps there was more to this encounter than mere coincidence.

In that moment, Aakash knew this was no ordinary meeting. He had stumbled upon something extraordinary. The stranger's words, though cryptic, resonated within him, urging him to dive deeper into his existence. He felt as if the key to life had been handed to him. He had been shown a door and it was up to him to walk through it.

Nobody had invested time to help Aakash see things beyond his immediate reality. His life had revolved around being stuck, but this one conversation left Akash hungry for more, not merely more knowledge, but a complete transformation. This time, Akash resolved not just to daydream about a better life but to actually build it.

5
Nishkām: Action without Fruit

'Why are you crying?'
'I once beat a dog to death,' the man confessed, breaking into anguished sobs.

Burying his face in his hands, he spoke between muffled sobs, 'but it is now that I realize...'

> *vidyā-vinaya-sampanne brāhmaṇe gavi hastini*
> *śhuni chaiva śhva-pāke cha paṇḍitāḥ sama-darśhinaḥ*
>
> Chapter 5, Verse 18

'What? What does that even mean? What happened to the dog?' Sattva cried out, his voice breaking into deep panic as his calm facade slowly dissolved. Sattva was perplexed—on one hand he wanted to reach out to console and comfort the man, and on the other he burned with a desperate need to know what had happened.

'It means,' the man said softly, 'that the one who is truly learned sees a Brahmin, a dog, an elephant and a dog eater with the same equal regard.'

Trying to wrap his young mind around the gravity of the man's words, Sattva asked innocently, 'So do you feel sorry for what you did?'

'I do,' the man replied, his voice filled with sorrow. 'Very much.'

Sattva realized in that moment that the man was crying not because of what he had done, but because of the guilt that consumed him, his thoughts.

Sattva, although just twelve years old, was led by an overwhelming need to help people. Hence he felt compelled to help the man feel better although he knew it wasn't his responsibility.

'Wouldn't that mean seeing yourself with kindness too? Please stop crying,' Sattva whispered, trying to soothe the man.

The man gave Sattva a weak smile through his tears, touched by the boy's compassion.

Suddenly, Sattva's attention snapped as an authoritative voice pierced through the air.

'Sattva,' his mother called out again. As he turned around to see what she wanted, he saw his mother entering the kitchen.

'What are you staring at in the mirror again? Come give me a hand here!' she commanded, her voice a mix of exasperation and anger.

'Every single day, it's the same. Just standing there, glued to that mirror. Why does he keep staring at himself so much?' she muttered under her breath.

'There is a man in the mirror, Ma. Come, look!' Sattva called out with a hint of urgency in his voice.

'Yes, and that man is you,' she retorted. 'Stop with your stories, Sattva. I have had enough of them. Come and help me now,' she added in a frustrated voice.

Ignoring his mother's call, Sattva turned back to the mirror only to find that the man had vanished.

All he could see in the mirror was his own reflection, looking at which a strange sense of emptiness washed over him like a sudden loss of identity.

Who was Sattva? He truly didn't know.

Who was the man he had seen in the mirror? He couldn't tell.

All Sattva knew was that every time he gazed into the mirror, he saw a different face, a different person, and heard a different story about a different suffering. Yet, when they disappeared, what lingered like a cloud over him was the same—confusion and chaos along with a flood of unanswered questions.

Who were these people? Was he imagining them? Was he delusional? Or worse, crazy? Could others see them too? I wish I knew. Each morning, Sattva asked himself these same questions, hoping to find an answer in the mirror someday.

Little did Sattva know he had been blessed with a strange and rare gift.

Since childhood, he had always felt a peculiar disconnect from the world around him. He had always felt 'different', without however understanding exactly how he was different.

So, day after day, he would stand in front of that mirror for hours, watching people come and go. People who were suffering and who would share their stories with him. He would speak with them and try to help them. Yet he could not decipher why he was seeing them. Or even whether he was helping them or if they were only a part of his imagination.

Today, again he kept gazing into the mirror. This time a woman appeared—she wore a knee-length dress with floral frills, not the fancy kind but the type Sattva had only seen in old movies. Her body seemed weak and frail, yet her eyes blazed with an undeniable fury that made her seem almost formidable.

Her eyes were unnaturally wide and her forehead was drawn into a frown while her lips were pursed with bitterness. The veins on her temples seemed to pop, indicating the pent-up aggression she carried within.

'You look upset, what happened?' Sattva enquired.

She looked at him with a cold, piercing gaze and then looked away silently.

He tried again. 'Tell me, what's troubling you?'

'My husband never gifted me anything luxurious. No fine jewellery, not even an expensive handbag to flaunt among my friends. They always waltzed in with their designer bags and expensive pieces of delicate jewellery that their husbands had gifted them, silently mocking yet showering me with sympathy. They thought I wouldn't notice their subtle smirks but I did,' she said, her voice trembling with restrained resentment.

'I worked tirelessly for that man—cooking and keeping his house in order, hosting perfect parties, standing by him during troubled times, and yet, not one expensive present?' she added regretfully.

Before Sattva could respond, he heard another voice—a calm, deep one this time that echoed from inside his own house:

> *ye hi sansparśa-jā bhogā duḥkha-yonaya eva te*
> *ādyantavantaḥ kaunteya na teṣhu ramate budhaḥ*

Chapter 5, Verse 22

Pleasures that arise from sensory contact with worldly objects are verily the wombs of sorrow; they have a beginning and an end. So the wise should not delight in them.

The woman in the mirror frowned at Sattva and disappeared. Sattva turned around to the source of the voice and saw Kannan, who had just responded to the woman in his mirror. Sattva stood there frozen and perplexed, caught in a whirlwind of thoughts that surged like a rising tide, leaving him mute and bewildered as Kannan offered him a gentle, knowing smile. They stood face to face, suspended in that moment.

Sattva wanted to speak yet found himself at a loss for words.

'Hello, sir. I hope you didn't have trouble finding our home? Please, come in,' Sattva's mother welcomed Kannan warmly and led him into the living room.

Still shocked, Sattva snapped out of his thoughts when he heard his mother call out:

'Please bring some water for *Sahab*,[4] Sattva,' she said.

In autopilot mode, Sattva stepped into the kitchen. He couldn't understand how the Sahab had answered the woman. Could he also see her? That would be the only legitimate

---

[4] Sahab: A polite title or form of respectful address for a man.

explanation. The thought that someone else was also able to see these people thrilled him. He felt excited to talk to this Sahab about it.

He entered the room and handed the glass of water to Kannan. He sat down next to his mother, quietly studying this stranger who perhaps shared his secret.

Finally, Kannan turned to Sattva and spoke to him kindly, 'Do you want to ask me something?'

Sattva shook his head quickly, still unsure.

Seeing this, his mother smiled, 'He is always lost in his own world.' She then turned to Sattva and said, 'Sattva, your Baba[5] is Sahab's driver. Baba has worked with Sahab for almost twenty years now. Last month, when your Baba expressed his desire to start a business someday, Sahab encouraged him and even agreed to provide us with a loan. As Baba is away on work, Sahab has come home. We need to thank Sahab.'

However, Sattva was still lost in Kannan's response to the woman in the mirror, for that meant that he too had seen and heard her. A wave of relief washed over him at this realization and he just wanted to speak with Kannan.

Meanwhile, his mother continued to speak. 'Pardon him, Sahab. He is always lost in his thoughts, barely paying attention to what's happening around him.'

'Oh! No need for an apology,' Kannan said with a soft smile. 'They are just kids with imagination, which helps them to dream bigger. We shouldn't disturb them. Right, Sattva?' he continued.

Sattva looked up and met Kannan's eyes. It was instantly

---

[5]Baba: Father.

clear to him that this man could definitely answer his questions.

◆

When his mother and Kannan had finished talking, Kannan rose to leave.

Sattva's mother gratefully folded her hands and thanked Kannan for the loan. She turned and quietly retreated indoors when Kannan headed out the front door.

Sattva seized this opportunity. Today was the day he had waited for since childhood—finally he would get answers. Slipping on his flip-flops, he called out, 'Ma, I am going out to play,' and dashed after Kannan.

Sattva caught up with Kannan in the narrow lane connecting their house to the main road, panting slightly.

'How did you know?' Sattva asked Kannan, breathlessly.

'Know the woman?' Kannan enquired.

'Yes, can you see them too?'

'Yes, I can,' Kannan nodded.

'I thought it was just me. I thought I was imagining it, or worse, maybe even...losing it,' Sattva explained.

'No Sattva, it wasn't your imagination and you are definitely not mad,' Kannan spoke gently to the young boy. 'You and I just share a gift. Everyone has one—most just don't know or are unable to identify it,' Kannan explained.

Kannan's calm tone offered some comfort, but Sattva's mind raced. The idea that only he and Kannan could see these people clouded his brain.

'Don't you think our gift is strange? Like it's not natural or it doesn't feel normal?' Sattva questioned.

'Weird? Maybe. But there have been many people on earth

who have had some superpower. Like Einstein, Ramanujan and Newton. Have you heard about them?' Kannan asked Sattva.

'Umm, no. Who are they?' Sattva asked, puzzled.

Kannan smiled. 'Hmm, alright, do you know your mother?'

'Of course. Why? Does she have a superpower too?' asked Sattva.

'Yes. She loves you selflessly. She even convinced your father to accept my offer so they can give you a better life. Is that less than a superpower?' Kannan asked with a head tilt.

'No, I never thought of it like that,' Sattva said, nodding slowly. 'So if their presence is not weird, then what do these people want from me? Why do I see them in the mirror? Each of them is either sad or angry or unhappy. I see their suffering. I feel so helpless knowing I cannot do anything for them. It breaks my heart,' Sattva finished with a sigh, seemingly carrying a weight on his shoulders.

Kannan looked at him thoughtfully and asked, 'Tell me, do you know what happens after death?'

'They either go to heaven or hell,' Sattva exclaimed confidently, proud to know the answer to at least one question that Kannan had asked.

'And what about those who go to neither heaven nor hell?'

Sattva hesitated, unsure. He looked confused but stayed silent.

'They roam the Earth troubled, in search of answers. They carry their unresolved questions, regrets, residual guilt or anger, all unfinished emotions. And somehow they believe you can help them,' Kannan continued.

'But I am just a kid. How could I help them? What could I possibly know that they don't?'

'Sattva, have you ever read the Bhagavad Gita?' Kannan enquired.

'My grandma used to tell me stories from the Bhagavad Gita when I was younger, but ever since she passed away I haven't read it,' Sattva answered.

Kannan smiled softly and then said something that Sattva didn't quite understand:

> *naiva kiñchit karomīti yukto manyeta tattva-vit*
> *paśhyañ śhriṇvan spṛiśhañjighrann aśhnangachchhan svapañśhvasan*
> *pralapan visṛijan grihṇann unmiṣhan nimiṣhann api indriyāṇīndriyārtheṣhu vartanta iti dhārayan*

>> Chapter 5, Verse 8-9

Kannan explained, 'Those dedicated to *karma yoga* live with a quiet detachment and maintain the perspective that "I am not the doer" even while performing actions like seeing, hearing, touching, smelling, moving, sleeping, breathing, speaking, excreting, grasping, and opening or closing their eyes. They understand that it is their material senses that are interacting with objects. They themselves remain detached.

'So essentially you are not the doer. You are just a means. A medium. Your duty is to accept and continue with your duty without the question of what it can bear you, as you are merely an instrument fulfilling a role without the expectation of reward or attachment to outcome.'

> *idaṁ śharīraṁ kaunteya kṣhetram ity abhidhīyate*
> *etad yo vetti taṁ prāhuḥ kṣhetra-jña iti tad-vidaḥ*

>> Chapter 13, Verse 2

The soul possesses no physical senses. It experiences the world indirectly through the body, mind and intellect complex, which are likened to its field of activities or 'field of energy' as modern science likes to describe this concept. Just as a magnet creates a magnetic field, the body serves as a field for the soul's activities and is termed as *kshetra*.[6]

'Though the soul is separate and distinct from the body-mind-intellect complex, it often mistakenly identifies itself with them. However, it remains the observer, aware of the body and is therefore called the *knower of the field*. You are that soul!

'Misidentifying with your physical body, mind and intellect, you take on its struggles and limits as your own. You attribute the limitations and suffering of the body-mind-intellect to yourself. You don't realize that limitations are part of the material world and subject to its influences and changes. As the soul you are beyond the world's control. Now how can a soul—eternal and free—truly have ego?'

'I'm still not sure I understand. What does this mean for me? I'm sorry if I'm asking too many questions but I feel you're the only one who can help me find some clarity,' Sattva said, with a shred of guilt.

Kannan laughed softly. 'Sattva, the answers you seek are already within you. I too am just a means, a signpost on your journey to propel you in the right direction. Come, let's have a cup of tea.'

---

[6]Kshetra: (Sanskrit) The field of activities.

Sattva had his reservations about the offer. He wondered what to do until Kannan said, 'We can talk about the people in the mirror too.'

Hearing this, Sattva immediately nodded and followed Kannan.

At the tea-stall, the world buzzed around them—a constant bustle from the street, vendors shouting, voices of passersby, people bargaining in shops, metal utensils clunking in the kitchen. These noises however faded as Sattva remained immersed in what Kannan was saying to him.

'Think of it this way—whenever something significant happens, good or bad, like winning an award or facing failure or hurting someone, we instinctively think "I did this". That's our ego speaking. It is natural for anyone to think he is the doer of an action. But more often than not we're all just the means, merely conduits for action,' Kannan continued.

'If no one is the doer, then who really is in control? Does it mean nobody is in control of what they're doing? Or that ultimately everything is, as Ma says, divine will? Or is God the doer?' Sattva asked, confused.

'It's not like that. Let's begin with the concept of *Triguna*, or the three fundamental qualities of nature that influence all beings. There are three *guna*s, one is your name itself, Sattva; the second is Rajas; and the third is Tamas. To know one's true self, one needs to understand these three gunas of *Prakriti* (nature)—Sattva, Rajas and Tamas—and how these three forces shape all thought and action,' Kannan said as he removed a pen from his pocket and drew something on a paper napkin.

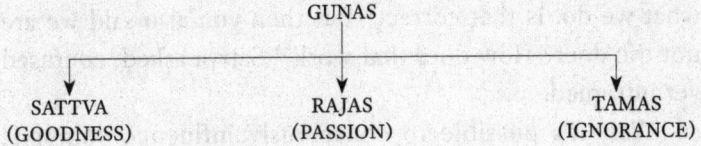

'The gunas are always present in every being. They are always in combination and never in equal measure. They ebb and flow, and within each one of us the percentage of these gunas keeps changing based on the situation we're facing. How we act in a particular situation is often shaped by whichever guna is most prominent in that moment. For example, when you engage in volunteer work or in selfless service for others without seeking anything in return, you are likely being guided by Sattva—the quality of purity and compassion. On the other hand, when you do something bad or destructive or act in ignorance, it implies that Tamas might be active. Rajas inspires activity, movement and desire,' Kannan said before explaining further.

'These gunas are present not just in people but in everything. They permeate nature and are present in seasons, days, food and time itself. For instance, the early morning hours around sunrise are predominantly influenced by Sattva, characterized by purity and clarity. As the day progresses, Rajasic energy takes over, characterized by activity and passion. By nightfall, Tamasic influence settles in, associated with inertia and darkness. Now what if I told you that you have the power to influence these gunas and actually create your own inner balance?' Kannan asked.

'That's possible? If we're able to create our own mix then in a way we can be in absolute control of how we act and what we do. Is that correct? But then you also said we are not the doer? How does that work?' Sattva asked, confused yet intrigued.

'Yes, it's possible to consciously influence yourself! Through food, habits, thoughts and the company you keep. These are the enablers that can help you to enhance a particular guna and help you to lead a life of your choice. But like I said, we are not the doer because the ultimate outcome does not lie in our control. We might be able to influence our internal reactions but we cannot control the external results,' Kannan said.

Sattva frowned slightly, still confused. 'Alright, look at it this way. Imagine that you studied really hard for your exams. You are confident of achieving good scores. Yet when the results came, you had barely passed. Has that happened with you?' asked Kannan.

'Yes, many times,' Sattva confessed.

'So despite your sincere efforts were you able to control the outcome?' Kannan asked.

'No, but I did my best,' Sattva said innocently.

'I agree, you did your duty. You studied well. Yet for some reason either you forgot the concepts or simply panicked during the exam. Whatever the reason, you were unable to control the outcome. Success or failure is never in your hands. Do you follow?' asked Kannan.

'Hmm. Yes, I see. You mean I can choose how to act or respond but never how it all turns out,' Sattva considered.

'Exactly. We can control what we think and therefore what we do and how we react.'

'How can I change the way I think?' Sattva asked, intrigued.

'Believe in the power of your thoughts. Thoughts are the predecessors of actions and a powerful force that can influence our lives in both positive and negative ways. Positive thinking can lead to abundance and success, while negative thinking can have equally strong but harmful consequences. Our thoughts are thus responsible for both our happiness and suffering. We may strive to improve our actions but our efforts can be hindered by impure thoughts,' Kannan explained.

'So how can I change my thoughts? They aren't something I can control,' Sattva asked.

'Yes, you can. I follow a methodology that can be broken down into four clear steps,' Kannan said as he went on to explain:

'Step 1: **Acknowledging.** This is something we discussed before. Acknowledging means facing your current reality. When you accept the situation and make peace with it, you can open space to think clearly and rationally of a way forward. This step is like turning on a light in a dark room. Accept your situation without sugar-coating it or running away from it. Just face it.

'Step 2: **Visualization.** This is a simple yet powerful technique where you need to visualize yourself where you want to be. Think of your mind as a movie projector. Every day play the scene in which you are exactly where you want to be. Picture yourself standing tall in a courtroom, confidently presenting your case—and winning. See yourself speaking clearly and boldly on stage, eyes meeting the audience without fear. The more often you replay these "mental movies", the more real they feel. Eventually, your mind starts to believe it. When the mind believes, the body follows. You will become what you think.

'Step 3: **Affirmations.** You can achieve what you have visualized for yourself with affirmations, which are like planting seeds. What you say to yourself daily starts to grow into your reality. When you say words like, "I am confident, I am capable, I can do this," the vibration of these words sends ripples through the Universe. You will then attract opportunities, people and energy that align with the words or affirmations that you repeat each day. It's the law of attraction at work. We attract what we think, what we say every day.

'Step 4: **Discarding negative thoughts.** Your mind is like a garden. Every time a weed shows up—"I can't do this, I am not good enough, or I am not worthy to deserve this"—pull up that weed and plant a flower. Replace that thought with a positive one. Soon you'll form a habit of thinking positive.

'Although we cannot control the outcome, we can take charge of our thoughts. We must realize that we are here to fulfil a role in life. Each one of us on earth is charged with a predetermined duty but most of us do not realize our true purpose. And even when we do, we attach it to an outcome. To satisfy our ego.'

'Ego? What exactly is that?' asked Sattva.

'It is a false identity we give ourselves. Remember that lady from the mirror? Her identity was built around being wealthy, surrounded by other richer women. That illusion fed her pride. That is why she was attached to the feeling of showing off and feeling proud about it. Her ego thrived on being seen as rich. But that identity was not real, it was only a mask,' Kannan explained before quoting from the Gita.

nādatte kasyachit pāpaṁ na chaiva sukṛitaṁ vibhuḥ
ajñānenāvṛitaṁ jñānaṁ tena muhyanti jantavaḥ

Chapter 5, Verse 15

'This verse suggests that the knowledge of the self is deluded by ignorance. Ignorance not just of who we are but even of our reality, purpose and our duty on this planet. So, ignorant souls strive to fulfil desires which only grow stronger with satiation, often converting to greed,' Kannan explained.

'And what if a desire does not get fulfilled?' asked Sattva.

'Then it converts into anger and frustration, clouding the intellect and deepening ignorance, just like that woman you saw in the mirror. In the physical body, the soul mistakenly identifies itself as the material person. It forgets its divine origin and eternal nature, associating with its human name, family and country. To satisfy bodily needs and seek material happiness, the living being engages in fruitless endeavours. Sometimes, knowingly or unknowingly, individuals commit sins to fulfil their materialistic desires. Do you understand?' Kannan asked.

'Yes, somewhat. So how can one detach from this cycle of ignorance and chasing desires, and just break free?' Sattva asked, his eyes wide with curiosity and eagerness.

It was a profound question for a twelve-year-old to ask. Kannan smiled, not at the boy's innocence but at the wisdom underlying his words.

'We must perform our duties without attachment to an outcome. We must act without the action feeding our ego or clinging to the fruits of our effort,' Kannan answered.

'How do I know if I am feeding my ego?' asked Sattva with disarming honesty.

'Again, a good question, Sattva,' Kannan said. By now, they had finished their tea and begun to walk back towards Sattva's home.

'Like I said, by not being ignorant to self. Introspection is the key. We must practise introspection with the thought that our ego is not our identity. It also means we must observe ourselves without judgement. Even face brutal facts about ourselves and look at them rationally without bias. We can learn to understand ourselves. Here is something I do. Whenever I feel I could have handled a situation better, I write it down. Then I think of the other choices I could have made. How could I have responded differently, more in line with my purpose. This simple practice helps me. It shows me where the ego took charge and how I could have kept it in check. It's a learning for the next time,' Kannan elaborated.

He continued in a deliberate voice, 'When you are led by a higher purpose, the ego begins to lose its grip as you are solely focused on the purpose. It takes work. It's a journey that can actually be categorized as a step-by-step process:

'Step 1: **Introspection.** Understand yourself, who you are. Journal your reactions, your desires, your needs, your personality, strengths, weaknesses and triggers. Be honest.
'Step 2: **Acceptance.** Face your reality and accept it.

Appreciate what you have. Don't chase an identity built on comparison with others. Like the woman in the mirror.

'Step 3: **Purpose.** Find your purpose in life.

'Step 4: **Detachment.** Detach from outcomes and results.

'Step 5: **Learning.** Fulfil your duty with utmost sincerity and keep improving along the way. Learn from each experience.'

By now they had reached the gate of Sattva's home. Kannan turned to the young boy who carried the load of others' sufferings on his slim shoulders, and said gently, 'Sattva, maybe it is your duty to guide these lost souls and help them find the answers. I do this for living beings I come across. Maybe your calling is similar. You must explore. Then you will know. Just remember one thing. Those who are ignorant chase their desires, which grow stronger, feeding the tree of material existence. Fulfilled desires grow into greed; unfulfilled ones turn into anger and frustration, clouding judgement and deepening ignorance, just like the woman you saw in the mirror. So just try to focus on fulfilling your duty. Do you understand?' Kannan asked.

Sattva nodded slowly.

Kannan smiled and bid farewell to Sattva as he gestured for him to go inside. Sattva walked into his home, lost in thought, questions swirling in his mind, but now they felt like the beginning of a new journey. As Sattva closed the door, he wondered when he would meet Kannan again.

6
Samatol: The Balance

'Doctor! Doctor, please wait,' Rama called out, breathless as he raced through the hospital hallway and struggled to catch up.

'Doctor, can you please tell me what's happening inside? How's my uncle?' Rama pleaded. 'No one is telling us anything. How is he doing?' he enquired in a voice raw with fear.

Rama's eyes darted through the emergency wing of the hospital, which was chaotic as stretchers wheeled past him and machines beeped rhythmically, the air thick with desperation and unanswered prayers. Doctors and nurses engaged in their daily hustle as families clung to hope.

The commotion mirrored Rama's headspace. He spotted his father and other family members huddled together outside the Emergency ICU where his uncle Rajesh was admitted.

Situated in the heart of Bijnor, in Uttar Pradesh, the hospital was the largest one in this small city and most reputed for its services. Naturally, Rama's family had brought Rajesh here for the best treatment. Rajesh wasn't just a prominent and respected businessman in Bijnor but also a significant member of the Gupta family. For Rama, he was not only a mentor but like a second father.

Rama felt numb, filled with fear. The doctor's sterile non-committal response did nothing to alleviate his anxiety. Rama's mind was stormy yet blank and spiralling, unable to process all that was happening.

He was fine yesterday, so what went wrong? How can it be so bad that he is in the ICU? Rama struggled for answers.

Rama's uncle Rajesh was much admired for his work ethic and commitment to the community and often cited as a living role model for the younger generation.

Rajesh had established multiple businesses and by the young age of 40 he had accumulated significant wealth—enough to magnetically attract the attention of every relative in the family who were suddenly drawn to him.

His wealth lured them in; they admired him not for who he was but for what he had. Their relationship with Rajesh was little more than a reflection of his financial standing and influential network.

However, Rama loved Rajesh unconditionally and fondly addressed him as *Chachu*[7]. The relationship they shared had nothing to do with Rajesh's wealth or status.

Rajesh had been an integral part of Rama's childhood and growing-up years—taking young Rama out on his bike for ice-cream treats, playing cricket with his friends in the park, telling him bedtime stories and even stepping in to shield him from his father's angry outbursts. For Rama, success never changed him. Rajesh Chachu was always there for him. Even

---

[7] Father's brother; uncle.

after Rajesh started working, he would make time each day to stay connected with what was going on in Rama's life.

'I want to be like you someday, Chachu!' Rama would say often. These memories played in his mind like a familiar tune on loop—comforting, vivid and real.

What had brought them closer was Rajesh's unexpected offer to Rama on his twenty-fourth birthday, five years ago. Hesitatingly, Rajesh had offered him the greatest gift—a place by his side in the business he had built from scratch. Rajesh had hesitated to make the offer because Rama was doing well professionally in his finance career, which he would have to leave to take a leap of faith with his Chachu. Rama's mind travelled to the day that had changed his life.

'Young man, you're twenty-four! Happy birthday, son,' Rajesh said, beaming with happiness as he hugged Rama.

'Thank you, Chachu! You know I usually don't ask for presents but twenty-four does seem like a good age to get one,' Rama said playfully, gently teasing Rajesh.

'As a matter of fact, I do have something for you this year,' Rajesh replied with a smile. 'And if you say yes, it would be a gift for me too.'

'I was only joking, Chachu. You never need a reason to get me anything. You always spoil me, whether it's my birthday or not,' Rama expressed with love.

'Rama, I've always seen a reflection of myself in you. You are hardworking, focused and always eager to learn. If I can play a role in helping you to hone your skills, I would consider it a privilege,' Rajesh said as he paused significantly, before adding, 'Would you like to join me in my business? We could build it together.' There was a glimmer of hope in

Rajesh's eyes. He had no family of his own and he considered Rama as his own son. So he wanted Rama to become his successor.

'Wow, Chachu, this is huge for me! I would love to learn from you and spend more time with you—this really is the best gift!' Rama said, his face lighting up with joy.

'Perfect, we shall discuss this tomorrow. Tonight, let's just enjoy,' Rajesh responded with a quick wink.

Since then, Rama had shadowed Rajesh, learning quickly, and soon begun to reliably manage all important tasks and payments.

And today, Rama felt helpless as he sat on the bench outside the ICU, adrift from reality. Rajesh had suddenly collapsed in his office without warning. No one knew what had happened. No one was even ready to tell him what was happening—Rama didn't know what to do.

The hours crawled by and relatives had started to trickle into the hospital. Rama remained rooted outside the ICU. He was not leaving his uncle's side.

Finally, late at night a doctor emerged.

Rama immediately stood up and asked, 'How is he, doctor? He is going to be okay, right?'

The doctor's face fell. 'You must be strong, son. He has multiple-organ failure. We have stabilized him for now so he can meet the family. But he does not have much time left. I am sorry,' the doctor replied. Rama's world came crashing down. He heard the one sentence he had dreaded hearing all day.

'I don't understand. How could this happen? He was fine yesterday,' Rama wept in disbelief, falling back on the seat behind him. His father held him as they hugged and wept together.

'I know how it feels, son. He didn't want you to know. He was suffering from liver cancer that went undetected until it was too late. *Dada*[8] was so occupied with work that he ignored all signs of the disease,' his father said.

The doctor came out of the ICU again and sensing Rama's distress, addressed his father, 'Mr Anil, you are Rajesh's brother, right? We will be shifting him to a normal ward now so he can meet everyone. I am sorry, we do not have any private rooms available,' he informed.

◆

Rajesh was shifted to the general ward and informed about his condition. He was calm and expressed his desire to meet Rama before the other relatives.

When Rama entered, trying to steady his breath, Rajesh stretched out his hand and asked the weeping young man to sit beside him. He caressed Rama's face and wiped off his tears. Holding Rama's hand, he said, 'Lying here in this sick bed waiting for death, I can recall the significant moments of my life. It has been a good life but I realize now that I have been a fool. I have been irresponsible with my health. Putting all my energy into work. All my wealth, achievements...none of them matter now. As death comes closer, I can only feel love and some regret.'

'No Chachu, I am sure we can still do something,' Rama whispered in a hopeful tone.

---

[8]Elder brother.

'No, you listen now. I want you to know that success is not everything.

'Relationships, passion, hobbies, dreams from your younger days are equally important, Rama. You will handle the business after me and I don't want you to repeat the same mistakes.

'I missed birthdays, family dinners, quiet evenings, moments that make a life whole. I can take with me not my wealth but only the memories created by love. So don't follow my path blindly, Rama. Chase meaning, not just numbers or milestones. Love deeply and freely. Take care of your health, your dreams, your people. These are the true treasures.' Rama cried silently as Rajesh continued in a resigned tone, 'Don't cry, my child. Everyone has to go someday. Just make sure you live life not with regrets, but with fulfilment. Life is beautiful when you cherish others. Do you understand me?'

Rama nodded, tightly holding Rajesh's hand, not wanting to let go. 'Good, now go outside and send in the others. Don't be sad. I shall always be with you,' Rajesh comforted Rama calmly.

Rama could see the regret in Rajesh's eyes—the regret of not starting a family, not spending time with those he cared about. And the feeling of helplessness in the face of death.

Rama slowly left the ward heavy-hearted, the weight of his Chachu's words pressing into his soul. He sent his father inside before sitting down on the bench, his eyes filled with tears. He still had some formalities to complete at the hospital.

Sitting with his own thoughts, he barely felt the hand on his shoulder.

Rama looked up and saw a man with long hair, calm eyes, and a face shining with empathy.

It was Kannan.

'Hey, are you okay? My name is Kannan. I was with my relative on the next bed and could not help hearing your uncle. I know nothing I say can fix this, but I am here and not every burden needs to be carried alone,' Kannan said.

Rama could still hear his Chachu's 'last words' ringing in his ears. Yet he found Kannan's presence strangely comforting and for the first time that day didn't feel entirely alone.

He looked at Kannan but remained at a total loss for words. All he could mumble was 'why'.

'Your uncle had been unwell for a long time. But he ignored the signs, buried as he was under work responsibilities,' Kannan said gently, settling down on the bench beside Rama. He then quoted a verse from the Gita:

nātyaśhnatastu yogo 'sti na chaikāntam anaśhnataḥ
na chāti-svapna-śhīlasya jāgrato naiva chārjuna

Chapter 6, Verse 16

'Balance, my friend. That's what your uncle wanted you to understand. Everything in life—work, rest, even dreams—needs to be lived in moderation. He had been unwell for a long time but he ignored the signs because he was too busy working. The body is our vehicle. So if the chariot is broken, how can we move towards our purpose? We need to take care of our body, otherwise how will it handle the ultimate burden of doing one's duty?' Kannan explained.

'How do you know this?' asked Rama.

'I overheard the doctors speaking. But it wasn't hard to see. He gave everything to the world except to himself.'

'But why him? Why does he have to die with regrets?' Rama asked.

Kannan paused, choosing his words with care. 'It is not just him. Even the greatest among us have regrets. Did you ever hear of Graca Machel?'

Rama nodded. 'Nelson Mandela's wife, right?'

'Yes. As a widow of the former president of South Africa, she once spoke about the sorrow Mandela had carried. When asked whether her husband had any regrets in life, she stated that he had never had enough time for his kids. You know that Nelson Mandela went to prison when his children were very young. His sorrow was not for the years he spent in prison or the sacrifices he made as a revolutionary, but simply for not being present as a father. He failed to balance his dreams with his personal relationships. His children grew up while he was behind bars. Of course he changed the world, but lost precious moments,' Kannan explained.

'How is his and my Chachu's story the same?' Rama asked.

'Well, both had regrets. Both were consumed by purpose but forgot balance. Both had something in common; they went too far in pursuing their professions. The Bhagavad Gita speaks of this too,' Kannan said.

yuktāhāra-vihārasya yukta-cheshtasya karmasu
yukta-svapnāvabodhasya yogo bhavati duḥkha-hā

Chapter 6, Verse 17

'One who is temperate in eating, balanced in work and recreation, and regulated in sleep and wakefulness—such a person finds yoga, which is all about balancing the mind and the body. It teaches about equanimity, accepting both success and failure with the same inner stillness. Yoga can help to eliminate suffering. I think your uncle was trying to teach you this lesson so you do not ignore the important things in life, be it your health or body or relationships. Don't become a prisoner of success,' Kannan elaborated.

Rama listened in silence. Kannan's words settled over him like gentle rain on parched earth. Just then, a nurse came out calling for Kannan. He stood up placing a reassuring hand on Rama's shoulder. 'You'll understand someday,' he said before he walked away.

Rama sat still, Kannan's words echoing alongside Chachu's. Deep within, he knew what they both were saying. He also knew that one day everything would make sense.

Just not today.

Today, Rama grieved.

7
Sankalp: Purpose Overcomes Fear

'Aarti, Baba's home. Please put the *tavah*[9] on the stove. Let's make some dinner,' Aarti's mother said from the other room.

Born in the small village of Lotwara in eastern Rajasthan, Aarti was the daughter of two daily wage earners who worked hard every day to make a living for themselves and their children.

'Already done, Ma! I know when Baba comes home,' Aarti replied with an innocent giggle lacing her words.

'You'll make a wonderful wife someday, Aarti. I am so proud of you,' her mother said as she entered the kitchen to start serving the food. Aarti's Baba and brothers had already taken their places in the dining area of the kitchen floor for dinner to start.

The kitchen was small, dim and cramped. The plaster on the walls had started to come off and spider webs were draped like lace in the neglected corners. There was miniscule

---
[9] A flat round pan or griddle used in cooking.

sunlight that flowed into the kitchen, which was still hot from the heat of the stove.

Even though the space was a little dingy, the house was always filled with laughter. The family ate together, chuckling about Aarti's mother's remarks.

Aarti flushed at her mother's words. Just that one word 'wife' tingled something in her as her cheeks turned a flaming red, a blush she could not hide.

Aarti's flashback broke just as suddenly as it had come. However, she could still feel the warmth of that moment—the feeling of anticipation and the subtle blush, even as the cold water crashed into her face, dragging her through the strong current of the Banganga river. She wanted to remember her last moments of freedom.

She felt as if she was drowning, submerged in the water, drifting in and out of consciousness. Every time she surfaced, as her vision cleared, a new memory took hold, like her entire life was flashing in front of her, unfolding scene by scene.

She had read somewhere that you could see your life flash in front of you at the time of death, yet this felt different. It felt like life was pleading with her to hold on. She wanted to enjoy every bit of her life story one last time before she drowned. 'Aarti will have to give up studying,' Aarti's father whispered in a low and hushed tone.

'That would break her,' her mother replied, distraught at this decision they were compelled to make.

Aarti had overheard her parents' conversation one night when they were discussing her future. Her family relied on manual labour to make ends meet and did not earn enough to be able to afford the education of all their children. She loved her brothers too much to take that away from them. So she gave up her books. It hurt but she had never complained.

She surfaced again. As she floated half-conscious, she felt weak. She wanted to give up struggling and just surrender instead, but her body would not stop fighting. Her willpower kept her afloat. Even as the river thrashed her body, for the first time in her life she felt free. She no longer had to pretend. She could just be. The cold water had numbed her wounds but when it washed over her, her arms burned and her back throbbed. Yet she felt free. She had managed to escape her sorrows and misery, at least for the moment.

'Hurry up, the *baraat* is here. We need to welcome them,' Aarti's father exclaimed in near panic.

It was Aarti's wedding day. The beating of *dhol*s, the shimmer of fairy lights all over the house, and a group of ladies singing happy wedding songs. All of Aarti's friends had danced as they shared her glee.

Aarti sat in a chair in front of the mirror draped in jewellery—gold and ruby necklaces adorned her neck, heavy earrings dropped from her ears. It was time for the veil to be placed over her head.

Aarti was in ecstasy. This was the happiest day of her life. She looked her best.

'Aarti, as a wife and daughter-in-law of the most prominent and influential family in the village, you must keep your husband and new family happy—that will give us utmost happiness,' her friends teased her about the wedding night, as Aarti blushed, hiding behind her veil and giggles.

Aarti was an average-looking homely girl with no dreams of her own. She had learned what her mother taught her

Sankalp: Purpose Overcomes Fear ◆ 99

and did what her brothers and father expected of her. She would find her happiness in whatever fate had in store for her. Her fantasy was simple—a husband, children, and a life rooted in love. She remembered the night she sat under the vast blanket of stars with the moon gazing down at her, wondering what her husband would be like. Would he love her? Would he be her best friend?

She wanted four children. Three sons and a daughter with whom she could discuss her life, just like her mother did with her. Although she was acutely aware her husband would be chosen for her, she was happy with the thought of being able to start a family. And then Thakur Sahab visited home.

She had been working at the farm. When she reached home, she saw villagers gathered outside her house. They spoke in hushed tones. 'Lucky girl,' she overheard.

When she entered home, she saw Thakur Sahab seated on a stool, as her mother served him some tea.

'Here she is, Thakur Sahab, my hardworking daughter. She works at the farm and helps me at home. She is a good girl,' her mother said.

Aarti touched Thakur Sahab's feet respectfully and headed to the kitchen to help her mother. In the kitchen, her mother hugged her and said, 'You are so lucky, Aarti. Thakur Sahab himself has come to ask for your hand in marriage for his youngest son, who has recently returned from the city.'

Aarti was shocked. She had never imagined a girl like her would catch the eye of the Thakur Sahab, the most influential man in the village. Why would he want to marry his son to her? Aarti knew she wasn't the prettiest girl around.

The questions swirled but she didn't question fate. She

decided to live in the moment instead. The life of her dreams was about to begin, or so she believed.

She again emerged from the river's icy grip, gasping for air.

Her heart ached with every thought of Nindra. She wanted to see her husband, her friend, one last time. One last look, one last hug, which she knew was impossible.

Nindra had died that morning. Though she had only known him for two months since her marriage, it was enough for her to love him. She drifted in the river's current, haunted by memories too tender to let go—the day of her wedding.

She hadn't seen or met the man she would marry. She was excited to finally see the person God had chosen for her. Her heart pounded as she walked to the *mandap*[10] imagining the silhouette of a strong and sturdy man in an ivory sherwani, a beautiful beard and a gentle heart.

With her first look at him, disappointment washed over her. She saw a man limping towards her. It was not a normal walk! It took her ten minutes to realize he had polio. His legs were weak and misshapen, and thin as bones.

Aarti felt betrayed. She shot a questioning glance at her mother, who looked down with a flash of guilt and a bowed head. She looked at her father and brothers and realized they already knew. They had kept it a secret from her. They had not had the courage to refuse Thakur Sahab.

She finally understood why Thakur Sahab had come home with a marriage proposal for a peasant girl like her.

She started to feel the burden of the extravagant jewellery she was wearing, all of which had been presented by

---

[10] A decorated altar for Hindu weddings.

Thakur Sahab's family. Thakur Sahab had three sons and she was going to be the youngest *bahu*[11] of the 'weakest' link in the family. Besides, considering her family background she quickly realized she would be nothing more than a maid to the family.

In that moment, she accepted her destiny and this twist of fate. Below her veil, her tears went unseen. She pulled herself together.

She knew the wedding ceremony was probably her last moment of enjoying attention and happiness. So she thoroughly enjoyed every moment of the ceremony as if it was for her alone.

Later, she found herself sitting on a bed, fully bedecked with flowers by her new sisters-in-law, who kept giggling. Aarti knew they were not laughing because something would happen inside the room tonight, but because there was a higher chance that nothing would.

Nindra entered the bedroom and sat beside Aarti. 'Hey, look at me,' he said in a soft, soothing voice.

She lifted her veil slowly and saw the man in front of her. He was so handsome. With chiselled features, his face was attractive. With strong shoulders, his upper body was well-sculpted. Had it not been for the polio, he would have turned the heads of many a woman. Yet she remained silent, weighed down by the sting of her family's betrayal.

Nindra spoke to her gently, 'With your silence, I am assuming you know nothing about my condition. I apologize on behalf of my father and yours too. My father can be really

---

[11] Daughter-in-law.

demanding but he always wants the best for his family. You too are a part of this family now. I am sure my father would have compelled your father. So please find it in your heart to forgive them both.'

She was taken aback. She was not expecting an apology.

He was not just handsome, but kind and wise too. She liked him.

Nindra continued to speak in a gentle voice, 'Please don't worry. I will do my best to make you feel at home. You're my wife and nothing will come in the way of you being treated with all due care and respect.' He offered her a smile as he placed his hand reassuringly over Aarti's.

A few hours earlier, Aarti had thought this man wouldn't even touch her and there would be only distance and duty. But here he was, speaking to her with grace, apologizing not just for himself, but also for the choices their fathers had made. It seemed surreal. Even her own father had never expressed remorse to her mother for the numerous mistakes he had made and continued to make. She realized then that Nindra was different and she could grow to love him.

She cherished his presence; they had become good friends and lovers. She started to love him and loved to care for him. She loved every bit of her day, starting from making his favourite meal to take to the office, to giving him a foot massage when he got back from work. Her affection extended to the entire Thakur family. They treated her with warmth and not any differently from the other daughters-in-law. She made a place for herself in the hearts of everyone. Thakur Sahab would fondly call her *choti bahurani* when she would scold him for not taking his medicines or forgetting to wear his footwear. She was truly happy.

But fate had other plans. Nindra suddenly passed away from an unknown illness. She woke up one day to find him lying lifeless next to her.

'Nindra! Wake up. Wake up. Open your eyes. Please talk to me,' she cried as she tried to wake Nindra from his slumber. But he remained still.

She rushed out of the room for help. A doctor soon arrived and announced that Nindra was no more. He said Nindra's polio-impacted poor immune response rendered him vulnerable to disease. His helpless voice confirmed what she refused to believe. Aarti crumpled to the floor, her world unravelling just when she had thought she would disclose the good news to everyone.

The shock and grief of losing her husband was too much for Aarti to handle. She was carrying her first child, who would now grow up without a father.

Aarti did not know then that her troubles had just started.

The Thakur family mourned Nindra's passing as they prepared for the last rites with full ceremony.

'Aarti, we need to tell you something,' Thakur Sahab said to her while everyone sat on the verandah around Nindra's lifeless body.

She looked up teary-eyed, unable to comprehend anything.

'The Thakur family is known for its deep-rooted tradition and rituals. Our integrity demands that we do what is right even in the toughest of situations. And today that responsibility falls on me. I intend to uphold this and I urge you to do the same,' he said firmly.

Aarti looked at Thakur Sahab silently, unable to predict

what he would say next.

'It is our tradition that when any man in the family dies, his wife becomes a sati. This practice has been followed for the last one hundred years. Today I shall honour my ancestors by upholding it,' he proudly announced.

She frowned at him blankly until his words sunk in. She was horrified and stood up in disbelief. Her wide-open eyes darted questioningly from her mother-in-law to her sisters-in-law. All looked down in shame, unable to meet her gaze.

Aarti fell to Thakur Sahab's feet crying, 'Papa, I am carrying his child. Your grandchild. Please don't do this.' She no longer remembered for how long she had cried and begged until Thakur Sahab walked away. She then pleaded with her mother-in-law, even her brothers-in-law, but no one listened.

She knew she was uneducated and belonged to a poor family, but she was certain that this *pratha*[12] was no longer permitted and definitely not when she was carrying an unborn child—all she had left of Nindra.

A strong current lashed against her, bringing her back from yet another scene in which her father had pleaded at the Thakur's feet for his daughter's release. Yet nothing had worked.

This was just hours before she had jumped into this river—desperate to save her unborn child from a fate far crueller than death. Even as the current tossed her like a leaf in a storm, fragments of her life surged through her consciousness.

---

[12]Custom.

Sitting in front of the fire in which she was going to be thrown, she faced a choice. Such customs, long accepted once, may have persuaded widows to submit without question. But today the world had changed. Men like Nindra would never have approved of this, neither for Aarti nor anyone else.

Courage is a tricky thing. Used at the wrong time or in the wrong place, it can be considered an act of foolishness. But when harnessed at the right moment, it can change lives for good. It creates the space to step back and to act upon your deepest convictions. It gives you the strength to leap and to break the status quo.

This is what Aarti did. As her in-laws led her towards the fire, she took that leap of faith. She didn't think whether she would succeed or fail, but she knew she had to try. She had to do it for her child, for Nindra, and most of all, for herself.

She didn't know where she found the courage from but in a split second she had grabbed the sword of one of the armed men and shouted, 'I swear on my Kanhaiya (Lord Krishna), I will not hesitate to strike down anyone who comes near me.'

'My child will live, Nindra's child will live. I will not have mercy on anyone who threatens this child,' she continued, eyes ablaze with defiance.

Stunned by Aarti's fury, everyone stepped back. Suddenly one of the men lunged forward and struck her with his sword that pierced her arm and then slid across her back. Aarti neither flinched nor cried out. She stood still for a second. Then driven by a cold fury, she turned and drove her sword directly into the man's stomach. He fell to the ground.

There was silence. Everyone present was paralysed with shock. 'You will regret this, Aarti,' her father-in-law said.

It was as if some unknown force had taken over Aarti. 'Really?' she laughed out loud, fearless, and glared at him with eyes wide with fury.

Everyone backed off as Aarti fled the scene with her sword raised threateningly.

The Thakur's men followed her as she ran. They chased her until she was backed up on a high hillside. She reached the cliff and looked down at the river below. Whether she jumped or not, the end was inevitable. She refused to die as a coward and swore not to go down without a fight.

This is what Nindra would want, she thought to herself as she sent out a prayer and made a leap of faith into the river.

She had been struggling in the cold waters of the Banganga River. The river threw her, thrashed her, pummelled her with its cold water, but kept her moving and alive. She remembered something her mother had once recited:

śhrī-bhagavān uvācha
abhayaṁ sattva-sanśhuddhir jñāna-yoga-vyavasthitiḥ
dānaṁ damaśh cha yajñaśh cha svādhyāyas tapa ārjavam
ahinsā satyam akrodhas tyāgaḥ śhāntir apaiśhunam
dayā bhūteṣhv aloluptvaṁ mārdavaṁ hrīr achāpalam
tejaḥ kṣhamā dhṛitiḥ śhaucham adroho nāti-mānitā
bhavanti sampadaṁ daivīm abhijātasya bhārata

Chapter 16, Verse 1-3

The Supreme Divine Personality said: O scion of Bharat, these are the saintly virtues of those endowed

> with a divine nature—fearlessness, purity of mind, steadfastness in spiritual knowledge, charity, control of the senses, sacrifice, study of the sacred books, austerity, and straightforwardness; truthfulness, absence of anger, renunciation, peacefulness, restraint from fault-finding, compassion toward all living beings, absence of covetousness, gentleness, modesty, and lack of fickleness; vigour, forgiveness, fortitude, cleanliness, bearing enmity toward none, and absence of vanity.

With these lines, she also used to tell her to be brave. We don't need to be free from fear; we just need a purpose bigger than fear.

Today Aarti had found her purpose. For as long as she could remember, others had defined her purpose. For the first time, she had made a conscious choice for herself that day and in doing so she understood the real meaning of her mother's words. Purpose could not be given, it had to be chosen, and she had decided to fight for her child's life, for herself and for Nindra.

She could not fathom where her strength had come from. It had just risen in her like an unstoppable tidal wave or a force of nature. Perhaps it was love.

At the cremation ground, her mother would have been proud of her, watching her daughter stand tall and unyielding, fuelled by a will larger than fear, fighting for the life of her unborn child. A sense of purpose could transform the fragile into a fierce force.

This was her final flashback before the water threw her near the riverbank, where the water was flowing more slowly.

Aarti could finally gasp for a free breath, which felt thin; her limbs felt heavy as darkness tugged at her invitingly. She felt weak but before she closed her eyes this time, she summoned every ounce of her strength and cried out for help. Perhaps someone might hear her, was her last conscious thought during this ordeal.

Moments later, dizziness swallowed her as she slipped into a slumber of darkness. Her body slackened and she was just about to surrender herself when she saw someone. At first she thought she was hallucinating. Or in a dream. He seemed familiar, but she did not know him.

He quickly leapt into the river, splashing through the water to reach her. He grabbed her arm and pulled her out from the water to safety. While doing so, he said in a voice that sounded eternal to Aarti's ears:

raso 'ham apsu kaunteya prabhāsmi śaśhi-sūryayoḥ
praṇavaḥ sarva-vedeṣhu śhabdaḥ khe pauruṣham nruṣhu

Chapter 7, Verse 8

I am the taste in water, and the radiance of the sun and the moon. I am the sacred syllable Om in the Vedic mantras; I am the sound in ether, and the ability in humans.

She felt like the Lord himself had spoken. A profound peace washed over her. She felt connected not only to the man who had spoken but to the Universe itself, to something vast and divine. The voice continued, deep and gentle:

daivī hyeṣhā guṇa-mayī mama māyā duratyayā
mām eva ye prapadyante māyām etāṁ taranti te

Chapter 7, Verse 14

Sankalp: Purpose Overcomes Fear

> My divine energy Maya, consisting of the three modes of nature, goodness, passion and ignorance, is very difficult to overcome. But those who surrender unto Me cross over it easily.

'You have overcome what most cannot across seven lifetimes. You have performed your duty, you acted without attachment, without wondering about the outcome. You were determined to do what is right and what was your purpose. You surrendered your will unto me. You, my love, will be liberated. You shall be safe,' the same soothing voice said to her.

'Who are you?' Aarti asked him in barely a whisper.

'Kannan, your saviour,' he replied.

'I am Aarti,' she said simply.

Kannan draped his jacket around Aarti's shivering shoulders. The cold water had numbed her wounds, nearly closing them. She sat still cocooned in the warmth of Kannan's jacket, slowly recovering from the storm within.

Kannan was explaining to her that he was returning after a visit to his patient, when walking by the river to the bus-stand he thought he heard a faint cry. He ran towards the sound and found her.

Seated on the riverbank now, he assured Aarti, 'Don't worry now, you are safe.'

She looked at him, eyes heavy with exhaustion and gratitude. 'Thank you for saving me. I had almost lost consciousness, and all hope too,' she replied, grateful for her new friend.

He nodded. 'What happened? How did you reach here? Did you slip into the river?' he enquired.

'No, I threw myself in it,' she replied.

Kannan's expression changed. 'Why, Aarti? What made you do it?' Kannan asked, concerned.

She took a deep breath and told him everything. As Aarti's story unfolded—raw, painful and full of courage—Kannan listened with utmost interest, spellbound by the strength it must have taken to endure it all.

After a long pause, he asked, 'What are you going to do next?'

Aarti looked at the river, its current calm now, like her. 'I don't know yet but I will do something to provide for my child. It is all I have got and honestly, right now I feel that I have been given more than I ever had. It may sound strange but it's like I have found myself. You and perhaps God, through you, have given me a new lease on life. It must mean something, right?' she replied.

'Yes, it does,' Kannan smiled, before asking her, 'Do you know what the self is called in the Bhagavad Gita? *Adhyatma*. In Sanskrit, it means the science of the soul. In the Bhagavad Gita, Lord Krishna refers to Himself as the integration of the Self—the body, mind, and intellect.'

tasmāt sarveṣhu kāleṣhu mām anusmara yudhya cha
mayyarpita-mano-buddhir mām evaiṣhyasyasanśhayam

Chapter 8, Verse 7

'This is what the Lord said to Arjuna. Whatever you do, keep your mind on me. Fight the war, do your duty. It means that no matter what you do, you must fulfil your duty, not for reward, not for outcome, but because it is yours to do. Do it without attachment to worldly output because control is an illusion,' Kannan said in a calm voice. Aarti sat there in awe, entranced by the music in his voice which had become the voice of the Universe.

8

Prakash: Light Within

Sometime in December 2012

'Svadhyaya'

It was a single word that flashed across hundreds of thousands of computer screens in India. Below this word there appeared a countdown that ticked ominously—cryptic and inexplicable. No one knew what it was, where it was headed or when it would stop. The countdown had begun five hours earlier, at 10 a.m., with 12:00:00 displayed on the screen. A countdown of twelve hours probably meant that something would be revealed at 10 p.m. The entire country was in a state of frenzy—it seemed like the biggest cyber breach of the decade, feeding into the widespread fear and hysteria that the world was coming to an end on 21 December 2012.

◆

The NEWS television reporter stated in the Breaking News programme: 'Most computers connected on the FAST private Wi-Fi network in India have stalled. Users are complaining that their screens have frozen and the machines are not working. Neither restarting the machine nor disconnecting from the network has worked. FAST officials stated that they are working on restoring clean connectivity. Users on other networks seem safe for the time being. FAST officials informed NEWS channel that technically a successful hack on a single device can be leveraged to other devices, thus compromising devices on the same network and potentially leading to a network-wide breach. Why have users on the FAST network been specifically targeted?'

Another television channel speculated on who was behind the cyber breach, while other channels ran popular conspiracy theories. There was panic, drama and confusion. Almost everyone seemed to be either directly impacted by the cyber breach or had lost their wits. It was surreal, like watching a satire unfold in real time. For the media it was news, for those in power an opportunity to push their agendas, and for the people whose screens were frozen with that mysterious word, the feeling ranged from uneasiness and disbelief to fear about losing vital data.

♦

Meanwhile, in the Human Resources department of a major multinational office in Connaught Place in Delhi, Anubhav questioned his co-workers, 'What do you think this countdown means?' He swivelled in his chair to face them.

'Whatever it is, it is big. I can feel it. Perhaps a message or a sign of the times to come,' said Kannan, who was a psychology major student at Delhi University and also worked as a marketing research intern.

'And who made you the team strategist, relying on your gut feel?' Prerna asked, chuckling. She was also an intern.

'Care to bet on it?' Kannan shot back, grinning from ear to ear.

'No, thank you. With laptops not working, does it mean we are off the hook for the day? We can do nothing anyway. A well-deserved day off, I guess,' Prerna said, and giggled.

'And you say that because...?' Anubhav asked, absently twisting and manipulating a Rubik's cube to rearrange a side into the same colour. He was quite good with the cube.

'No laptops means no work,' Prerna answered with a shrug, settling into a chair.

By midday, the trio and almost everyone in the office had spent hours staring blankly at their screens or ordered coffee and taken a walk outside as the countdown ticked down from twelve hours to seven hours.

Staring fixedly at his laptop screen, Kannan took out his phone to search the meaning of the word Svadhyaya that was displayed on the screen.

It was a Sanskrit word that basically meant self-study. Meanwhile, on television, NEWS channel had brought in a Sanskrit scholar who was explaining the meaning of this word:

'Svadhyaya is a compound Sanskrit word composed of sva (स्व) + adhyaya (अध्याय). *Adhyaya* means "a lesson, lecture, chapter; reading". *Sva* means "own, one's own, self, the human soul". Therefore, *Svadhyaya* literally means "one's own reading, or lesson".'

'Thank you, sir. Stay tuned viewers, until we return from the break with more information on this master hacker.'

'Even now, all these channels are merely speculating. They only care about their TRPs.[13] This could be a serious threat,' Prerna exclaimed, slightly worried now.

'Hmm. What happened to your "no laptop, no work" logic?' Kannan enquired, with eyebrows raised.

'The truth is, everyone looks out for themselves no matter the situation. So there's no need to make such a big deal about it, you two,' Anubhav advised.

In the background, the news blared from the television screen.

'In a major turn, we have learnt that the Supreme Court has intervened to direct the CBI to investigate the hacking incident. Even the police is on high alert. Cryptographers are already trying to decode the message flashing on screens across the country. Our in-house astrologer suggests that one of the cycles of time is ending as per the ancient Mayan calendar, which could mean that the world is going to end on December 21, 2012. Maybe this hacking is a precursor to the doomsday prophecy,' the reporter announced gravely, apparently unaware about the waves of panic the news could unleash amongst people.

'Did you hear that?' Prerna asked.

'What?' Kannan enquired.

'They are saying there could be a bigger underlying threat. We are in the centre of the city. Should we be heading

---

[13]TRP: Television Rating Point is a metric used to measure the popularity and viewership of television programmes.

home?' Prerna asked, clearly worried now.

No one had a response to her question. Yet, most of them felt they were safe until the clock struck 10 p.m. Meanwhile, Anubhav learnt that the office had to be evacuated immediately. To everyone's relief, he ordered everyone to head back home.

All of them left the office in a rush, including Kannan.

◆

When Kannan entered his house, he found his grandfather sitting in his favourite chair, flipping through news channels trying to find any new information.

'All these channels are saying the same thing. Useless noise,' his grandfather chuckled.

'*Dadaji*, do you know what this word *Svadhyaya* means?' Kannan asked.

'I do,' Dadaji said, and paused before continuing. 'It reminds me of a verse from the Bhagavad Gita.'

jñānena tu tad ajñānaṁ yeshāṁ nāśhitam ātmanaḥ
teshām āditya-vaj jñānaṁ prakāśhayati tat param

Chapter 5, Verse 16

'It means that truth is revealed for those whose ignorance is dispelled by knowledge of the self—like the sun, illuminating everything under its gaze. To them knowledge unveils the Supreme,' Dadaji explained.

'But Dadaji, do you really think this incident connects with the Bhagavad Gita? I mean the news is calling it a precursor to the end of the world. Moreover, what could one achieve by flashing something from the Bhagavad Gita on multiple screens across the nation?' Kannan asked, his curiosity peaking.

His grandfather shrugged. 'I don't know. The word just reminded me about this verse, so I shared it with you. That's all. Anyway, did they send you back home early because of this incident?' Dadaji asked.

'Yes, the situation has spiralled. However, what did you mean by knowledge revealing the Supreme? What exactly is the Supreme? How is it revealed by Knowledge?' Kannan asked.

Kannan's grandfather had known his grandson to be an insatiably curious child, always wanting to know more, bombarding him with questions about the forces of nature, the mysteries of life, what the universe was made of, and everything in between. It was almost impossible to say anything to Kannan without being ready for a follow-up question.

So instead of directly responding to the question, *Dadaji* quoted another verse from the Bhagavad Gita.

*puruṣhaḥ sa paraḥ pārtha bhaktyā labhyas tvananyayā
yasyāntaḥ-sthāni bhūtāni yena sarvam idaṁ tatam*

Chapter 8, Verse 22

The Supreme Divine Personality is the ultimate reality, greater than all that exists and the source of all existence. The Supreme is all-pervading and everything exists within Him. He is not easily recognized or understood. Devotion, or bhakti, is the key to understanding and realizing the personal form of the Supreme.

Dadaji paused before continuing, 'Both knowledge or *jnana*

that dispels ignorance and devotion or *bhakti* are distinct but interconnected pathways to reveal and realize the Supreme being. While knowledge illuminates the true nature of reality, devotion nurtures a loving relationship with the divine. It is only through devotion, through keeping your mind on God while performing your duty and your day-to-day activities, that you can attain him. True devotion is not in renunciation but in remembrance.'

Kannan loved these long discussions with his Dadaji about the Bhagavad Gita. He would listen, learn the verses by heart, and question the deeper meaning underlying each chapter. This was their usual practice.

They spoke for hours sitting in front of the muted television, discussing different concepts about *karma*, *dharma* and the soul from the Bhagavad Gita. Both did not realize how fast time had passed. Until Kannan suddenly glanced at the clock. It was already 9:45 p.m. The countdown on the laptop now showed only 15 minutes.

What would happen? News anchors braced for impact. Studio lights dimmed and dramatic music played. Speculation was rife. The network provider had not yet been able to decipher the source of the hack. Across the country, people waited with open laptops. Just like Kannan. They had no choice but to sit back and see what would happen. Then the clock struck 10.

Immediately, the screen flickered as the countdown beeped down to zero with a loud ring. Kannan saw the word *Svadhyaya* disappear from the screen and another message popped up. It said:

samo 'haṁ sarva-bhūteṣhu na me dveṣhyo 'sti na priyaḥ
ye bhajanti tu māṁ bhaktyā mayi te teṣhu chāpyaham

Chapter 9, Verse 29

I am equally disposed to all living beings; I am neither inimical nor partial to anyone. But the devotees who worship Me with love reside in Me and I reside in them.

Instantly, Kannan recognized the message as another verse from the Bhagavad Gita. It essentially called out to everyone and stated that God is partial towards no one. The message hung in the air like a direct challenge to humanity.

Then the screen shifted. An image of a young boy wearing a mask appeared. He looked lean, slight and almost fragile. Silence blanketed the room. Across the nation people held their breath.

And then the young boy spoke. His voice was also masked and sounded tinny, as if coming from a far distance.

'I am nobody. I come from a small town. I belong to a scheduled caste. We are still regarded as untouchable. All my life, I have been denied education. Even when I used to sit outside the village classroom just to hear what the teachers were teaching, I was always shooed away. Every time, I heard the same words: "How dare you enter the grounds? Polluting everything and everyone around you. Go away!" These words became the soundtrack of my life.

'Please tell me, what was my fault? It wasn't my choice to be born into this caste, destined to remain uneducated and labelled as an untouchable. No one in my family or in my community was educated enough to teach me. I ask you, what kind of society do we live in even today. A society that clings to ancient hate? Discriminates against people? How does hate help society? I remain uneducated and untouchable. Yet I have hacked all your computers. I've created a code which even your "genius" service providers cannot override.

'I gave you 12 hours during which you perhaps experienced fear. This helplessness you faced today has been my entire life condensed into half a day.

'Imagine waking up each morning knowing you have the talent, the intelligence and the skillset but no path ahead. No door to knock, no hand to reach out for.

'I am as capable as any MIT graduate. I possess the skills demanded from top-level engineers in the best multinational corporations. However, I do not have a degree, no formal education and no paper to prove my worth or change my life. And yet here I am, openly holding you to ransom but demanding nothing in return. I do not seek revenge for the injustice meted out to me; just your reflection. I want to ask you: When God himself does not discriminate, who are you to do so?'

The boy then quoted another verse from the Bhagavad Gita:

māṁ hi pārtha vyapāśhritya ye 'pi syuḥ pāpa-yonayaḥ
striyo vaiśhyās tathā śhūdrās te 'pi yānti parāṁ gatim

Chapter 9, Verse 32

All those who take refuge in Me, whatever their birth, race, gender, or caste, even those whom society scorns, will attain the supreme destination.

'I will see you in heaven some day. Because there you and I will be the same. Don't even think about looking for me. You will never be able to trace me. Not even after having seen me and heard me. I promise you this.'

The screen suddenly went dark. There was silence. Even the news anchors went quiet for a moment as computer systems across the country automatically rebooted. Normalcy was restored as if nothing had happened.

Kannan and his Dadaji sat motionless, the glow of the television reflecting in their eyes. They had listened attentively to the words of the young boy. Dadaji broke the silence.

'You know Kannan, that boy's story...it's not unique. Most of us are discriminated against in some form or another. No one really asks us what we want. People only think from their own perspective. Rarely do they try to step into another's shoes. That's why they fail to understand, and worse, they fail to care.' Kannan's grandfather sighed.

'Why does no one do anything about the rampant discrimination in our society, Dadaji?' Kannan asked, barely twenty-four at the time.

'Did you?' his grandfather shot back.

'I never thought about it,' Kannan admitted innocently.

'It is not your fault. Our society conditions us to want to succeed. We are trained on how to succeed in life; how to behave appropriately with others; how to get good marks; how to get a job; or even about the importance of earning money. No one teaches us about the importance of serving others, or how to be empathetic towards others, or even how to make a life and not just a living. In reality we are ignorant beings, a society of educated minds and uneducated hearts,' Dadaji explained.

Kannan frowned, puzzled. 'Isn't it obvious, Dadaji? I mean, take that boy for instance. Why should he have to suffer for being born in a particular caste?' Kannan questioned.

'It is obvious to you, Kannan, but not to those who benefit from the system the way it is. The greed for personal gain lies at the root of the problem,' Dadaji said, and paused to recall and speak another verse from the Bhagavad Gita.

ichchhā-dveṣha-samutthena dvandva-mohena bhārata
sarva-bhūtāni sammohaṁ sarge yānti parantapa

Chapter 7, Verse 27

O scion of Bharata, O conqueror of the foe, all living entities are born into delusion, bewildered by dualities arising from desire and hate.

Dadaji continued, 'The concept of untouchability did not emanate from reason. It was birthed by those who had the desire to wield control, to dominate others. Attached to this desire and the power it brought, there was anger from which sprung delusion and ignorance. Blinded by their desire and hate, they judged others for their background, mistakes, habits or any reason whatsoever. Even years later, the world doesn't ignore the truth because it's hidden. It ignores it because it's inconvenient and that situation is more dangerous.'

Kannan remained thoughtful. 'So, tell me Dadaji, what about the more petty stuff? There is this person in my office for instance, who always speaks negatively. He criticizes others and judges them if they are even a few minutes late.

He bickers and complains about the small stuff. What does he gain from it?' Kannan asked.

Dadaji nodded. 'Perhaps he is insecure about his own position. Maybe he desires recognition for always being punctual. Or perhaps he just wants to feel in control. However, this is all speculation, Kannan. You just need to understand that any desire for material objects or any desire rooted in the ego, hate or resentment will lead to ignorance. It pulls us away from clarity as well as peace, and sets us back many steps on our journey of self-realization. Remember, we must react less, understand more,' Kannan's grandfather elaborated.

This wisdom hit a chord with Kannan. For the first time, he saw himself clearly. He realized that like so many others he never went beyond the surface to understand the deeper truth, to ask why about a person or a situation. He too was quick to judge—like a pebble tossed across a lake that skipped across the water, one quick bounce after another, never sinking to the depths. He realized that often he did not do enough.

That evening something changed in Kannan. He initiated a journey to stop being ignorant. He promised to see, to understand, and to be present for others.

9
Nishchay: Steadfast Within

'Hello, sir. How are you?'
'I am good, who's this?'

'Sir, I'm calling with some great news. You have won a brand-new Honda City car in the lucky coupon you filled out last week.'

'What? Wow! This must be my lucky day! How do I claim it?'

'It's simple, sir. You just need to submit a down payment of ₹1 lakh. We shall take care of the rest. I am sending you a copy of the lucky coupon confirming your win from the company.'

'Oh, I see.'

'The car is worth ₹8 lakh, sir. As a lucky draw winner, you only need to pay ₹1 lakh. We will share all the documents with you and handle all the paperwork.'

'Alright, please share the documents. How do I make the payment?' Maryam soon shared the relevant documents, answered some more queries from the surprised winner and having convinced him, soon accepted the payment.

Maryam vividly recalled this conversation while sitting across from a Human Resources executive in a large multinational company.

Sitting in this chair, Maryam was poised to take a decisive step towards a new, changed life. Her heart raced. She was scared. Fear gripped her, not of rejection but of not being understood, especially about why she had done what she had to do.

'Maryam, you support a family of seven, right? Including your mother and five sisters?' the HR executive enquired.

'Yes, ma'am. One of my sisters is soon to be married. I hope to arrange it this year. That's why I need this job,' Maryam replied eagerly, her eyes filled with a quiet desperation.

'Where does your family stay?' the HR executive continued questioning Maryam.

'In Assam, ma'am.'

Maryam belonged to Nalbari, a small city in Assam, where she lived with her family. Her father had passed away when she was still a child, leaving her mother to raise six daughters while being the sole breadwinner for the family. Naturally, Maryam as the eldest had to soon start working to support her family and ease her mother's burden. She had found work in a call centre in Assam.

'What made you decide to relocate when your family is still in Assam, where you hold a job?' the executive asked, genuinely curious.

'Ma'am, I want to live a clean life with dignity,' Maryam replied with complete honesty.

'I'm sorry, I don't understand. Can you please explain?' the executive was confused. This was the first time someone had given her an abstract answer of this kind.

Maryam took a deep breath. 'Ma'am, I used to work for a company that scammed people every day, tricking them into giving up their hard-earned money. For every ₹1 lakh I extracted, I received a ten per cent cut. It was quick money and I needed every rupee. When people eventually discovered that they had been scammed, I am sure they cried. Some may have even cursed me. But I had a family to feed and I convinced myself that I had no other choice.

'Eventually I couldn't do it anymore. My guilt consumed me. I could not sleep at night. My conscience finally forced me to leave the job. I decided I would rather struggle honestly than thrive through deceit. Yes, living in the city is going to be more expensive and I'll have less money to send home but at least I'll earn it with integrity,' Maryam said with a very serious look on her face.

The HR executive sat in silence, visibly moved. No candidate she had interviewed had ever spoken to her with such raw truth and disarming honesty. Finally she spoke, 'I don't know what to say. You have been incredibly brave. But if you don't mind me asking, you were in that job for three whole years. What made you finally walk away?'

Maryam smiled faintly. 'One conversation,' she replied.

♦

It was a slow, quiet Saturday morning at Maryam's home. She was off work and had woken up late. She drifted into the kitchen from where a delicious aroma of breakfast wafted through the air. Her mom and sister were busy at the counter.

'What are you guys making today? It smells so good!'

Nishchay: Steadfast Within • 127

Maryam asked, giving her mother a sleepy hug.

'*Jolpan*, your favourite!' her mother replied. 'Tea is already on the table. Help yourself and let me know if it needs reheating.' *Jolpan*, a traditional Assamese breakfast prepared with rice, lentils and fresh vegetables, was a comforting start to her day.

Maryam poured herself a cup of tea and wandered into the living room. 'It's still hot, Ma. Thanks,' she called out, picking up the newspaper as she settled into the sofa.

She began flipping through the pages mindlessly at first, until an image caught her eye. It was the photo of a woman, bruised and battered, probably beaten up, sitting desultorily on a hospital bed.

The caption below read: 'Bela Nath, 36, was brutally assaulted by her husband.'

A chill crept up Maryam's spine. 'Could it be her? No, no...how could it? I am just overthinking it,' she thought to herself, shaking her head. But she was unable to turn the page and continued to read the accompanying article.

GUWAHATI, ASSAM — Bela Nath, a 36-year-old woman, was admitted to Assam Medical College and Hospital following what authorities described as a severe domestic assault.

According to the police, Bela Nath is being treated for multiple injuries after being allegedly attacked by her husband, whose name has been withheld pending formal charges. Police sources said he had become increasingly abusive after losing significant monies in a financial scam. He claimed that his wife, Bela Nath, was responsible for the loss as she had forwarded the scammer's call to him. 'He's deflecting blame,' said Inspector Rajiv Sharma. 'Regardless of the circumstances, this is a clear case of domestic violence, notwithstanding the scammers' racket in Assam,' he added. The incident adds to growing concerns about the widespread scamming operations currently targeting residents across Assam.

Medical authorities confirmed that Bela Nath's condition was stable, though she remained under observation. Police are investigating the assault and the fraudulent scheme that allegedly precipitated the violence.

Social workers highlighted this case as another tragic example of the complex relationship between financial stress and domestic violence. Residents are urged to report suspected scams to cybercrime units rather than handling financial frustrations through destructive behaviours.

Maryam froze. Bela Nath. The name was familiar. She was one of the people Maryam had recently scammed. It hit her like a strong punch in the gut as she realized that she had caused this woman's suffering.

Maryam suddenly felt disoriented. During three years of conning people, Maryam had never paused even once to reflect on the impact of her 'work', or its consequences on the victims. She had only thought about her own family. For her, the money meant survival.

But this? It was too real. This woman is in the hospital because of me. How could he do this to her? Maryam thought to herself. How many others have suffered because of me? Oh God! What have I done! Maryam battled with her thoughts.

She barely noticed her mother who entered the room with a plate of hot breakfast for her. Maryam was lost in her own miserable world, barely listening to her mother.

'Maryam! I have been calling you. What's wrong? Are

you even listening?' her mother asked in a slightly annoyed tone. 'Maryam!' she called out, louder this time.

Startled, Maryam returned to reality and looked at her mother, her eyes full of guilt, shame and fear.

'*Beta*, are you okay? What happened?' Maryam's mother asked, clearly concerned about her daughter.

Without a word, Maryam picked her bag and rushed to the door.

'Where are you going, Maryam?' her mother called out behind her.

'I will be back soon,' Maryam shouted, already halfway down the stairs leading out of the house.

Maryam just knew she had to visit the hospital. She had to see Bela Nath and the damage she had caused. If God graced her with an opportunity to apologize, she must.

◆

The hospital seemed shrouded in a low and dark stillness. Sickness and grief clung to the air in every corner. Nurses rushed by, doctors tended to their patients busily writing instructions on their clipboards, and every now and then another patient arrived. Even though it was a small hospital, it had every amenity—except solace.

Maryam approached the front desk. 'Bela Nath is a patient here. Which ward is she in?' Maryam asked, with as much courage as she could muster.

'What is your relationship with the patient? Are you another reporter? She is in no condition to meet anyone,' the receptionist said without looking up, her eyes never once leaving the register in which she was busy writing.

'No, I, umm, I'm her friend. I just want to check how she's doing now,' Maryam replied, her voice faltering.

The receptionist sensed Maryam's hesitation and immediately looked up to give her an odd look, trying to read the truth on her face. Ultimately, perhaps assuming that the domestic violence had made her uneasy, she relented.

'General ward, bed 109. Go straight and then turn right,' the receptionist directed Maryam.

Maryam nodded and walked briskly, heading for the general ward, her eyes scanning the hospital for both Bela and the police.

As she approached the ward, Maryam's pace slowed. She saw Bela from a distance, lying motionless on a narrow bed, almost lifeless. Her face was swollen. She had bruises under her eyes, along her jaw, near her ears. Both her arms were swathed in bandages with deep cuts visible on her hands. She looked fragile, broken.

Maryam's heart filled with guilt and shame. Her legs felt weak. Tears welled up in her eyes as she started to sob, seeing what she had caused. She wanted to fall at Bela's bedside and apologize, beg for forgiveness and repent. But her legs wouldn't move. She was rooted, not by guilt, but fear. *If I go to her, this won't end well. I will be dragged into the police investigation and questioned. They will trace this incident to me,* Maryam thought.

'My apology isn't going to fix this. If the police catch me, my whole family will be ruined,' Maryam whispered, trying to convince herself that an apology was not going to make it better for Bela. Yet deep down she knew it was a lie.

Just as Maryam turned around to leave, a voice broke the silence behind her.

'I'm sorry. Were you saying something to me?' a tall man with long hair, wearing a white coat, asked her.

Maryam flinched. 'Umm no, sorry. I am just leaving,' she muttered, almost panicking at the sight of this doctor who had spoken to her.

The man studied her face. 'Hold on, you look rather rattled. Is everything okay? Can I bring you some water?' he asked.

'No, I'm fine. I need to leave,' Maryam replied quickly as she started to edge towards the door.

'You know I heard you mention an apology,' the man said from behind her.

Maryam froze in her tracks. She knew it was over for her now. The doctor knew.

The doctor stepped closer and in a kind voice said, 'Sometimes we carry the guilt of things we never meant to happen or their consequences. It's not unusual.'

He gestured down the hall. 'Come, let's take a short walk. You look like you could use some water,' he continued.

Maryam followed, not because she trusted him but because leaving abruptly would raise suspicion. She knew she didn't have a choice.

As they walked, she asked, 'You mentioned something about carrying the guilt for things we don't mean to happen. How do you know what guilt I'm carrying?'

He smiled softly. 'It was easy because you said your apology won't fix this. That usually means someone's hurting and thinks that what happened is either their fault or they did not intend for the consequences,' the doctor replied. He then gave Maryam a glass of water and pulled up a chair.

Maryam stared at him, somewhat confused. He didn't sound like a doctor. Doctors didn't speak to strangers and when they did, it was only about medicines and diseases. So who was he? She thought to herself as she took a seat opposite him.

He caught her look and said, 'I'm Kannan. I'm a temporary psychologist here at the hospital filling in for another doctor for a month. My work is a little different from the usual medical doctors. It's my job to understand what people actually mean when they say something. Hence understanding what you said and felt was textbook for me.'

'Oh! I'm Maryam,' she replied meekly.

Kannan studied her. Evidently, Maryam was a woman at war with herself. She seemed to be fighting an internal battle.

'Would you like to talk about what happened?' Kannan asked.

Maryam didn't speak but just looked down. He observed that she was picking at her nails, tapping her foot nervously, all signs of anxiety, confusion and fear.

'Anything you tell me, however bad, stays between us. It's called doctor-patient privilege,' Kannan said with a reassuring smile.

Maryam's eyes shone with hope. Perhaps she could speak with Kannan and get some clarity about her situation—her desire to accept her mistake and make things right without police involvement. Yet fear held her back. 'Even if I did something very wrong?' Maryam asked.

'Yes, whatever you did would just stay with me, Maryam,' Kannan said reassuringly. 'We all make mistakes. What matters is what we do next. How we choose to make it right. Owning up the mistake is half the battle and signals the desire for a clearer conscience,' he added in his gentle voice.

Maryam felt she could trust him as he would listen without judging her. She wanted to come clean. 'I work for a company that scams people,' Maryam said, her voice shaking. 'We call people and tell them they have won a car lottery and in order to redeem it, they need to pay a small fee. And then we disappear,' she said.

Kannan nodded. 'What's in it for you?'

'I get a ten per cent cut from each deposit that I bring to the company, which is good money,' she replied in a small voice wracked with guilt.

'How much do you make in a month?' he asked.

'A lakh, sometimes much more,' she replied.

'So why are you here?'

Maryam looked down, tears streaming from her eyes. Mustering courage, she said, 'A patient admitted here was beaten up by her husband when they lost money in the scam that I facilitated. I recognized her name in the newspaper report and immediately set out for the hospital to see her.'

'Hmmm. Are you content with your work? Knowing that your income feeds your family but ruins someone else,' Kannan asked.

Maryam was trembling. She had never given any thought to the repercussions of her work or the ripple effect of her actions. She had been too ignorant.

'No,' she whispered. 'I used to think that they were rich and would just be sad for a few days. I never imagined it could...it would lead to this,' she said.

Kannan leaned back, listening. He kept quiet.

'Are you trying to make me feel worse?' Maryam snapped, her voice cracking. 'Because I already do. I never meant for this to happen. I have just realized today that I may have destroyed not one but many lives. I didn't know I was hurting others, Kannan. I am not a bad person,' Maryam blurted out in anger, crying incessantly. There was desperation in her voice, an urgent need to be forgiven.

Kannan sighed. 'I believe you,' he said quietly.

aham ātmā guḍākeśa sarva-bhūtāśhaya-sthitaḥ
aham ādiśh cha madhyaṁ cha bhūtānām anta eva cha

Chapter 10, Verse 20

'Do you understand what this means, Maryam?' Kannan asked gently, his voice kind and thoughtful.

She shook her head.

'I believe God resides within each of us, so whenever I speak with anyone, I remind myself that I'm addressing Him. That's why I try never to speak harshly. After all, how could I be unkind to Him? I see that divine spark in you too, Maryam, regardless of the choices you've made or your current path,' Kannan continued, leaning forward slightly, his voice soft and sincere.

He paused, then continued with quiet conviction. 'We all carry our burdens, our own struggles and unspoken stories. I don't know what led you into this work and I won't judge you for it. I speak with you now with an open heart seeking to understand, offering you the same compassion I'd offer anyone else. Everyone deserves that chance to be truly seen.'

Maryam remained silent. A storm raged inside her—guilt, fear, sorrow and terrible shame. She had expected anger, accusations, even condemnation from Kannan, but he was still calm. Still kind. She sighed.

'I know now that I have made mistakes. I feel guilty for my actions yet helpless. I didn't choose this work for pleasure or greed but soon I liked the comfort that money brought. Then my mother developed some health issues and now I am completely responsible for my family. I have no fancy degree or skills to earn as much money by any other means. This is the only way I know. I fear being fired or having to leave this job. I hate feeling powerless at the prospect of having no money to spend,' Maryam replied, unable to take charge of her emotions.

Kannan listened intently. Then he said, 'I understand you feel trapped, Maryam, but you are not powerless to chart your path ahead. This feeling of helplessness doesn't arise from your external circumstances, it comes from surrendering your inner strength, your mind and your soul.' He paused, then quoted thoughtfully:

manaḥ-prasādaḥ saumyatvaṁ maunam ātma-vinigrahaḥ
bhāva-sanśhuddhir ity etat tapo mānasam uchyate

Chapter 17, Verse 16

Serenity of thought, gentleness, silence, self-control, and purity of being—these are the true austerities of the mind.

Kannan explained further, 'Our mind is like a garden that can be either cultivated with care or neglected to grow wild.

A wise gardener not only nurtures the beneficial plants that yield fruits and flowers but also vigilantly pulls out the weeds that could choke their growth. Have you heard this before?

'Watch your thoughts, for they become words; watch your words, for they become actions; watch your actions, for they become habits; watch your habits, for they become character; watch your character, for it becomes your destiny.'

Kannan paused. He looked into her eyes and said, 'Maryam, I urge you to assess your finances and material requirements and then reflect not just on your needs but your character, your impact on society, your purpose and your duties. Is this job truly aligned with who you truly are and who you wish to become? Remember that those who feel perpetually trapped are often enslaved not by others but by their own desires and impulses.

'True liberation doesn't come from money or security. It comes from disciplining the mind. From freeing yourself from fear and cravings that drive the endless pursuit of pleasure or the desperate need for quick money. When you are truly free, you will stop feeling trapped—not because the world has changed but because you have,' Kannan paused and looked at her.

Maryam understood. Her voice trembled as she said, 'I don't know how to undo the pain I have caused, Kannan. I don't even know how many people I have hurt. But I know I need to do something.'

Kannan nodded. 'What you have done cannot be changed. But what you do next after today is up to you. I can only show you the direction. You have already taken the first step by accepting the consequences of your actions. You must therefore know that this job is not who you are or what you want to be. That, in itself, is freedom.'

yo na hṛiṣhyati na dveṣhṭi na śhochati na kāṅkṣhati
śhubhāśhubha-parityāgī bhaktimān yaḥ sa me priyaḥ

Chapter 12, Verse 17

Those who remain unmoved by both worldly joys and sorrows, who neither grieve for losses nor crave for gains, and who have renounced both good and bad deeds, such devoted souls are especially dear to Me.

'The choice is yours,' Kannan concluded.

◆

'This conversation with a stranger gave me the clarity and the courage to change my direction and want to live responsibly,' Maryam said, sitting tall before the HR executive.

10
Anitya: This Too Shall Pass

'Great, just great! Could this life get any better?' Mira frowned glancing up at the ominous dark clouds and the pelting rain and then down at her jeans soaked halfway to the knees.

The monsoon had been merciless all week. Roads had turned into rivers, traffic slowly inched forward determinedly, pedestrians treaded carefully with their umbrellas even as the capital city that usually did not see much rain had become a minefield of waterlogged potholes.

Mira stood beside a rusted tea cart near the metro station, clutching her half-broken umbrella and a backpack stuffed with design books borrowed from the community library. The library had been the singular constant in her life over the past three weeks. Her job at the boutique firm was gone, her savings were drying up, and Rishi, who had once promised her forever, hadn't returned a single call in eleven days. He was either ghosting her or had blocked her number.

The tea vendor handed her a small cutting chai. Mira took the tiny cup and leaned back against the only dry spot on the wall behind her. That's when she heard someone beside her say, 'Rain's got a PhD in bad timing, doesn't it?'

She turned to see a man in his late thirties in a dull blue kurta with an elegantly draped scarf over his shoulder. He had kind eyes, the sort that looked like they'd seen things and didn't flinch. A calm in the storm.

'Bad timing, huh? Ask me about it! This rain seems like the lesser of the evils in my life right now,' she said before she could stop herself.

The man smiled. 'You sound like someone who's lost her umbrella and her patience, in that order.'

She looked at him, amused despite herself. 'You got the sequence right. Except you missed the job firing, the heartbreak and the unpaid bills.'

'I am sorry to hear that,' he said, sipping his tea. He offered his hand. 'I'm Kannan.'

She shook it. 'Mira.'

They stood near the chai vendor watching the rain continue to flood the street. Mira was quiet for a bit. She didn't usually open up to strangers but today she didn't feel the need to guard her words. She felt different.

'You know, I used to believe that by thirty, I'd have it all figured out. Now I think I will die unsuccessful,' she said.

'Funny thing about life, it prefers cliffhangers over conclusions,' Kannan replied with a gentle smile.

As the rain eased to a soft drizzle, they walked together towards a bus stop just across the street. It provided better shelter. It was also empty with only a stray dog napping under the bench seeking refuge from the pouring sky.

Mira was as exhausted as if she had been holding her

breath for weeks. She needed to vent and who better than this kind stranger whom she was unlikely to meet again. She let it all spill out, no holds barred.

'My team manager fired me. He said my ideas are too indie for our clients, whatever that means. All I did was suggest innovative designs that were not cheap rip-offs of their competitors. I had genuinely put my heart into building those concepts but originality was too risky for the client. No one wants to stand out,' Mira vented with a heavy sigh.

'I understand. Can't you find another job?' Kannan asked.

'See, it is not hard to obtain freelance work. I already have some work lined up. The problem is getting paid. Clients take months to clear invoices and payments get stuck. I am constantly juggling cash flow with rent and bills to pay. Do you understand what I am dealing with?' she asked politely.

'Yes, I do. It sounds frustrating,' he replied.

'Yes, it is. Now I am also covering my mom's hospital bills. She is a single parent with health issues and relies on me. She tries to not have to lean on me but what to do? She does not earn too much,' Mira was just getting warmed up.

'And then there is Rishi. My boyfriend, no sorry, my apparent boyfriend who hasn't returned my calls over the last eleven days since I told him I wanted to introduce him to my mom. I thought we were ready to talk about marriage. Perhaps the "M" word was too scary for him. He has vanished into thin air. No response to my calls or messages. Just silence. What happened to basic courtesy, Kannan? Don't men have the courage to break up face to face? Even a break-up text would have sufficed. Something like, "Hey, sorry. I don't think it's working out between us, so I am kind of over it—wish you the best." Is that too much to ask?' Mira said.

'Not at all. I agree. There is dignity in communicating your feelings honestly,' Kannan replied.

'And then there is my mom. She is on a mission for me to marry. She wants me to settle down in life—which is fine. I want to as well. But does she need to remind me every day that I am thirty and still single? Like I am not trying. I thought Rishi was the one and now I am too weary to start over. Even the rain has not let up and today morning my umbrella broke. This is all just too much to take now!' Mira poured out her sorrows to a kind ear.

Kannan listened. Not the polite, glazed-over kind of hearing. He actually listened. Then he said, 'Sounds like chaos. Would you mind hearing something? This may seem a little out of context at first, but trust me, it'll make sense.'

Mira raised an eyebrow. 'What is it? Are you going to give me the same *gyaan* of giving life a chance and that it will all come back together?' She said in an impatient, frustrated tone of voice.

He laughed, a warm sound of genuine amusement, and then said, 'No, Mira, absolutely not!'

'What is it then?' she asked, curious.

'Would you want to know what the Bhagavad Gita says about chaos like this?' he asked.

Mira blinked. 'Isn't that like...religious?'

He chuckled. 'Let's just say that it's more like a user manual for people pretending to be in control.'

He recited aloud:

mātrā-sparśhās tu kaunteya śhītoṣhṇa-sukha-duḥkha-dāḥ
āgamāpāyino 'nityās tāms -titikṣhasva bhārata

Chapter 2, Verse 14

O son of Kunti, the contact between the senses and the sense objects gives rise to heat and cold, pleasure and pain. These experiences are fleeting, they come and go. Endure them bravely.

'What you're feeling—this sadness, the anger, the self-doubt—it's all real. But it's not permanent,' Kannan explained.

Mira crossed her arms. 'So I'm just supposed to sit around and wait for the Universe to stop messing with me?'

'Not wait,' he said. 'Understand. The Gita doesn't say "don't feel". It says "don't cling". Joy and sorrow—they're just visitors. Let them pass through. Just don't offer them permanent residence.'

She gave a dry laugh. 'You sound like my therapist but with better metaphors.'

'Well, I am a psychologist if that qualifies,' he laughed.

'Really? You sounded so calm and I kept wondering why. Now I know,' she said.

'My calmness has nothing to do with my profession. You can be calm too if you have the right approach,' he said, with a slight head nod.

Mira sighed. 'How can I do that? I could really use some calm and stability in life. I feel like I am stuck, or worse, shrinking with every passing day. If that's even possible,' she confessed.

Kannan smiled. 'Then this might help.' He then quoted

another verse from the Bhagavad Gita.

jātasya hi dhruvo mṛityur dhruvaṁ janma mṛitasya cha
tasmād aparihārye 'rthe na tvaṁ śhochitum arhasi

Chapter 2, Verse 27

For one who is born, death is certain. And for one who has died, rebirth is certain. Therefore, you should not lament over the inevitable.

Mira narrowed her eyes and stared at him. 'That sounds... dark.'

'Or liberating,' he said. 'Depends on your perspective. What you're going through—it's ephemeral. It's a cycle. This low will pass too, just like your last high and the one that follows. So why let either state own you or define your present?'

'Our body is equipped with five senses—sight, smell, taste, touch and hearing. Every time these senses interact with the world, they create experiences—sometimes pleasurable, sometimes uncomfortable. But here's the truth: none of those experiences last. They rise and fade, just like the seasons.' He leaned back slightly, pausing to let the idea settle.

'Cool water feels heavenly on a summer day but touch that same water in the middle of winter and you will flinch. The water hasn't changed—the context has. Pleasure or pain, they are both fleeting. If we allow them to control us, we'll spend our whole lives reacting or bouncing from high to low, never steady,' Kannan stated.

Mira was listening closely now.

'Someone who learns to observe these feelings without

being consumed or ruled by them—that person doesn't sway. They don't chase every joy or fear every pain. They remain anchored and clear. Grounded and calm,' Kannan said.

Mira looked thoughtful. By now, the rain had begun to lighten to a mild drizzle.

'You really believe this?' she asked.

Kannan nodded. 'Every word. Because I've lived it. I have lost jobs, lost people and even lost my purpose. But each time, I held on to one truth: This too shall pass. This is not exactly from the Gita but speaks to me in the same spirit.'

'So you don't think I will die unsuccessful?' she blurted out, and instantly winced at how foolish it sounded.

Kannan looked at her gently. 'Let me ask you something. Are you afraid of dying?'

'I am,' she admitted. 'I am afraid of dying without achieving what I set out to do,' she clarified, wondering whether she was saying the right thing.

Kannan nodded. 'Let me tell you a story about the Pandavas:[14]

'During their exile, the Pandavas were one day wandering in the forest, when they felt thirsty. Shortly they came across a well. Yudhishthir asked Bheem to go and fetch water for all of them. When Bheem reached the well, a *yakṣha*—semi-celestial being—spoke from inside the well. "I shall permit you to take the water only if you answer my questions first." Bheem paid no heed to the voice and proceeded to draw

---

[14]Pāṇḍavas, from the Indian epic Mahabharata, were the five warrior brothers who were victorious in the great war with their cousins, the Kauravas.

water from the well. The *yakṣha* pulled him in.

'One by one, Arjuna, Nakul and Sahadev went to fetch water—but each ignored the warning of the voice from within the well. Each of them was pulled in. Finally, Yudhishthir arrived. He listened to the voice and agreed to answer the questions. The voice belonged to Yamraj, the god of death, in disguise.

'One question he asked was: "What is the most surprising thing in the world?" Yudhishthir replied: "People die every day and yet they live as if they will never die. What could be more astonishing?"'

Kannan looked at Mira and said, 'Why lament over things that are inevitable? Why worry about things that you have no control over? Might as well do your best in any situation and make it worthwhile. That's all any of us can do, isn't it?'

They stood in silence for a moment, watching the rainwater flow past their feet like time itself.

Mira turned to him, 'So what do I do now?'

He shrugged. 'You breathe. You do the next right thing. You keep showing up. And one day, without realizing it you'll smile and not know why. That's when you'll know you've passed through.'

Mira smiled, just a little. 'You should present on TED Talks.'

Kannan looked at his watch and jumped. 'Speaking of talks...crap, I'm late!'

'Late for what?' she asked.

'I'm supposed to give a talk at a youth centre nearby. On the Gita, of course. The rain messed up my schedule.'

He started to walk away, then paused and turned back. 'You want to come for the talk?'

Mira blinked. 'Me?'

'Yes. You've already experienced the trailer. Might as well see the full film.'

She considered it, then nodded. 'Lead the way, *guruji*.'

Kannan laughed. 'Let's stick with fellow commuter in the rain.'

11
Purnahuti: A Return to Self

Kannan arrived at the Youth Centre with Mira. Rain still clung to him; his blue kurta was almost soaked, as was his scarf.

'Hey Mira, why don't you go ahead and take a seat. Let me dry off a bit before the speech. I shall catch up with you soon,' Kannan said, running a hand through his damp long hair.

Mira nodded and turned to scan the auditorium for a convenient seat. She was amused with herself at having followed a stranger and ending up at this centre, which felt oddly fated.

Maybe everything happens for a reason, she thought, settling into a nearby seat in the left wing from where the stage was clearly visible.

She looked around. It was a big auditorium, holding close to 500 seats and already buzzing with the murmur of an eager audience. A lot of people seemed to have turned up despite the weather, to hear Kannan. He must be compelling—so many people wouldn't show up otherwise, she mused. Just then, a woman beside her asked, 'Do you know Kannan?'

'Yes, we just met,' Mira chuckled.

'He does have that effect on people, doesn't he?' the woman smiled.

'How do you know him?' Mira asked, curious.

'We met at the airport and then we were on the same flight. I am Aayesha,' the woman responded warmly.

'Hmm, I am Mira. It's a pleasure to meet you, Aayesha,' Mira replied as they shook hands.

◆

In the right wing of the auditorium, just three rows from the stage, Aanyahi and Raya sat together, deep in conversation about why neither was keen to get married.

Raya, with an eye on the people now streaming into the auditorium, veered from topic and broke the discussion by asking Aanyahi, 'Does Kannan do these speeches often?'

'Yes, he is good at them and genuinely loves to reach out to others through these talks. For him, it is yet another way to influence lives, perhaps even transform them,' Aanyahi replied.

'Classic Kannan!' Raya said, and both of them chuckled knowingly.

◆

'This way, Papa,' Rama said to his father, gently guiding him through the auditorium doors. The day his uncle passed, Rama had met a stranger who spoke to him kindly. He knew nothing about the man until much later, scrolling through Instagram one evening, he stumbled upon one of Kannan's podcasts and recognized the voice.

Kannan seemed to be an influential persona on social media with a powerful voice and Rama had been quietly following him ever since.

When he found out that Kannan was speaking at a public forum in a nearby city, he immediately booked passes for himself and his father to attend the event.

He felt like he could use some of Kannan's clarity and calm. His uncle's demise had left him to deal with some pain and too many dilemmas. He didn't know if Kannan's speech would help him, but he remembered the calm Kannan's words had brought him. He was hoping to receive some of that peace again. For himself and his father. They found seats in a middle row of the central wing, midway down the hall.

◆

In the front row of the central wing, Aarti sat quietly, eagerly waiting for Kannan's session to start. Her eyes gazed at the stage but her mind was elsewhere—back to the day when Kannan had saved her and her unborn child.

Since then, she had lived in an ashram Kannan had recommended. She had found a job that paid her for sewing clothes. For the first time in years, she was free—free to make her own choices, free to live. She was happy. And soon, she would bring Nindra's child into this world.

Kannan had personally invited her for this talk and she had instantly accepted.

Next to her sat a woman whose face was disfigured with deep scars. Yet she sat tall, unafraid, exuding confidence. Aarti glanced at her with quiet admiration.

◆

A short distance away from the auditorium, Aakash's cell phone pinged. A message for a food-order delivery. One sandwich with a side of fries. Pick-up: Ravi's cafe. Drop location: Youth Centre.

Aakash glanced at the notification, hopped on his motorbike and headed to the café. Another delivery, another customer. He picked up the order, cheerfully greeting the café owner who sat at the till.

He whistled as he drove his 'new' second-hand bike to the delivery location. As he entered the Youth Centre, he noticed a large number of people, most of them in groups, with some murmurings about the Bhagavad Gita. That's when his eye caught a glimpse of a prominently displayed banner with Kannan's face on it. That's him! The man who brought me to the hospital, spoke to me and even paid for the food delivery I could not make, Aakash thought to himself as he parked his bike and walked to the delivery location backstage. He met the customer, someone named Om, and delivered the food packet.

'Hey, do you work here?' Aakash asked Om.

'Yes, I am the speaker's assistant,' Om replied.

'I know him. Kannan helped me once,' Aakash said.

'Yes, that sounds like Kannan, always ready to help others,' Om said with a smile.

'Do you think I could stay back with you to hear his speech?' Aakash asked innocently.

Om hesitated, then nodded. 'Yes, of course, why not.' Om did not want to shoo away a young impressionable boy like Aakash. Besides, Kannan would have liked Aakash to stay. 'Kannan always says, never stop anyone from learning about the Bhagavad Gita. It has the power to transform lives!' Om said to Aakash.

Pleased and grinning, Aakash sat on the floor near the curtains where Om was working. Peeking out, he could see the packed auditorium filling up with more people.

He saw a large group of professionally dressed men and women walk into the hall. Everyone was in formals. Aakash could see that this was a team of office-goers from a multinational company.

Among them was Maryam. She had recently landed her dream job as part of the company's marketing programme. Her team had been invited to attend Kannan's talk. Like Aakash, Maryam too was surprised to see Kannan's face on the banner.

It's him! The psychologist from the hospital, she realized. What are the odds? What a small world! Maryam thought to herself as she settled down in her chair, somewhat stunned by this turn of events marking fate's strange symmetry.

◆

The crowd settled when the host stepped on stage. 'Good afternoon, everyone, and welcome. It is wonderful to see this determined audience that has made it to this event despite the rain. Thank you so much for being here. We are certain that each of you will leave here with some valuable takeaways,' the host said as a ripple of anticipation moved through the hall.

'Allow me to introduce our speaker, someone who truly doesn't need any introduction...' the host continued. Laughter broke out as the host went on, 'Kannan is a renowned psychologist and an established speaker with a humungous following on social media platforms. He hails from Delhi and has spent the last eleven years travelling through the length and breadth of the country, transforming lives through pursuits such as personal counselling, podcasts, digital content, live sessions, and more recently though his bestselling book *Beyond Fear*. Please welcome him to the stage!'

Applause erupted as Kannan stepped forward and stood with folded hands to thank the audience. The host handed him the microphone even as the applause continued. Kannan smiled and began to speak.

'Thank you, my dear friend, for such a kind and generous introduction. And a heartfelt welcome to each one of you gathered here today.

'It's an honour to be speaking before you all, some familiar, some new. But all drawn here by something deeper than coincidence, something powerful nudging you to be here in this moment.

'I am Kannan, a psychologist working at Safdarjung Hospital and a professor at Delhi University. My purpose, my dharma, is to help people find direction—clarity that leads to understanding the true essence of Yoga. Be it karma yoga, the path of selfless action, or bhakti yoga, the path of heartfelt devotion, my duty is to ensure that the truth is told and knowledge is shared to awaken the light within.

'As I look at all of you, I see modern-day Arjunas—each of you standing in your own chariot, caught in your own battlefields of the mind. Just like him, your thoughts clash like swords, fear looms like a shadow, and varied desires pull you in countless directions. A war is waged every day.

'And all this turmoil stems from one question: what will

happen next? You are perplexed about what you stand to gain, what you will conquer, what you will lose. None of us present here know what this very hour holds for us. Or what the next moment shall bring.

'So I ask you to first close your eyes. Breathe deeply, freely, as you are meant to. Let go of fear, just for the duration of this talk. Breathe with me. Let's take five deep breaths, one by one, together. Let the breath be your anchor. Breathe.'

Everyone breathed together. With Kannan, under his direction and spell.

'Breathe deeply from your stomach...and gently let it out. Perform this simple activity with neither attachment nor gain. Expect nothing. Simply breathe because action performed without attachment to reward is the highest form of action. Just like a mother selflessly cares for her child expecting nothing in return yet offering everything.

'By embracing just this thought, you will have already taken one step away from ignorance. From this single step emerges the promise of a happier, peaceful and more meaningful life. This wisdom is as applicable to you today as it was to Arjuna millennia ago.

'Open your eyes.

'When we perform an action only in the hope of a reward, we tend to be driven by passion—what the Gita calls "*rajasic*". These rewards are elusive, which means that passion might or might not bear the fruits you expect. Such is life. It does not play by our rules and often disappoints when we cling to expectations. The fundamental truth is this: we are not in control of the results of our actions. We can only control the quality of effort.

'Now, someone might ask, "Kannan, if we cannot expect results, then shouldn't we renounce action altogether? Why work when we cannot expect what we want from an action?" Let me answer this not with an opinion, but scripture. Let me quote from the Bhagavad Gita.'

na hi deha-bhṛitā śhakyaṁ tyaktuṁ karmāṇy aśheṣhataḥ
yas tu karma-phala-tyāgī sa tyāgīty abhidhīyate

Chapter 18, Verse 11

It is impossible for an embodied being to completely renounce all activities. But one who renounces the fruits of action is truly considered a renunciant.

'Let me ask you: can you give up breathing, seeing, hearing, sitting or standing? These too are actions. Hence, no one, absolutely no one in this world, can completely renounce actions. What one can do is give up attachment to outcomes or the fruits of our actions. Today, more than ever, in our chaotic world with hectic lifestyles surrounded by social media, juggling multiple jobs to sustain ourselves, this ancient wisdom becomes even more relevant.

'Let's take a contemporary example. Social media is an essential element of our modern world. Are there any content creators here?' Kannan enquired.

A couple of hands from the audience went up.

'You there—tell me, my friend, why do you post content?' Kannan pointed to someone who had raised their hand. He requested an assistant sound technician to pass the microphone to the person in the audience.

With the mike in hand, the man spoke, 'I post because I

want to be an influencer. I like to show the world what my life looks like. It makes me happy, especially when others view the reel and post their comments or emojis.'

'Yet, how do you measure success? How do you know if you're doing a good job?'

'I see a rise in my followers when my reels do well,' he said.

'Yes, but how do you control whether someone taps the follow button or moves on to the next reel?' Kannan asked.

The person fell silent.

'That's the point,' Kannan continued.

'You cannot control whether others will follow you even if they like your content. What you can control is whether your content adds value. Create not to be liked or rewarded for it but to genuinely help others. Don't measure success by whether your reel is watched by ten people or even ten million—ask yourself whether you have offered something meaningful. That is karma yoga in practice—performing your duty with integrity and without attachment to results. Don't let attachment cloud your thinking, be it attachment to results, recognition, appreciation, or even to material objects, wealth or status. Such delusions darken the intellect,' Kannan paused and looked at his audience before continuing.

'While entering this building, did any of you notice a man begging for money right outside the main door. His name is Nandu. He is from a well-to-do family. He was educated and even respected at one time, until addiction to alcohol consumed him. He traded his house for another bottle. His ability to discern right from wrong dissolved. His intellect became shrouded in darkness—what the Gita calls "*tamasic*" intelligence, where the light of wisdom is completely lost in the fog of attachment and desire. Attachment to materialistic gains weakens us just as it weakened Arjuna. His attachment to his kin, his concern for their material well-being, blinded him to his duties. Battling with this profound dilemma, he was ready to abandon his duty.

'Anyone who can discriminate between right and wrong, actions that should be embraced or renounced, and understands what deserves to be feared or ignored, possesses "*sattvic*" intellect and gains true liberation.

'Today you might think that I'm here to teach you how to be happy in life. You might even think I can convince you to choose your own happiness by letting go of attachment. But that's only part of the truth and I would be deceiving you if I stopped there,' Kannan paused.

The audience listened raptly, yet somewhat confused.

'Confused? Let me explain. I might convince you that you can be happy by renouncing attachment to results, but what if I tell you that true wisdom lies in understanding that you're not even in control of that choice? A person free from ignorance understands that emotions, while natural, are material experiences. Thus, the ability to renounce the attachment to outcomes also means being able to treat both happiness and sorrow as equal. The wise are able to treat both extremes of duality as the same, like bravery and fear or even joy and pain, that rise and ebb like the waves in an ocean. Remember, you are not the wave, you are the ocean.

'Your body and mind create an illusion that makes you believe you are the ultimate doer. They foster ego. But it is with your soul—your true self—that you must connect.

What you must contemplate is how to unite with your soul. The ego-driven self that claims "I am the doer" is an illusion created by your material existence. This false self experiences the pleasures and pains inflicted on your physical and mental form. But your true soul transcends these temporary experiences. The ancient philosopher Epictetus wisely said, "Most of us would be seized with fear if our bodies went numb and would do everything possible to avoid it, yet we take no interest at all in the numbing of our souls." A disconnected soul takes one away from their authentic self. When you're not connected with your true nature, you try to find happiness outside yourself. And as I mentioned before, external sources, life circumstances and other people will disappoint you because your expectations are built on shifting foundations.

'True happiness stems from your soul, your inner self. It's not dependent on external circumstances but arises from alignment with your authentic nature. So ask yourself: Who am I? What values do I hold, independent of role or reward? What is my purpose, beyond survival and success or the roles I play? When you regularly ask yourself these questions, you'll begin to know your authentic self. The journey of reconnecting with the soul, of shedding the ego, is where lasting peace lies.

'The path forward is not to escape action but to act with complete dedication while remaining unattached to results. Perform your duties as offerings, not as transactions. Give your best effort as a gift to the world, not as a bargaining chip for personal gain.

'My friends, consider me your charioteer today, just as Krishna served as Arjuna's guide. Allow me to point you toward the path of righteousness and virtue, not because I have all the answers but because sometimes we need someone to remind us of the wisdom we already carry within. The battlefield of life will continue. The choice is whether you'll fight with attachment and anxiety, or with clarity and peace. With fear or faith? Will you act for gain or will you serve with grace? Karma yoga is selfless action. It is not about becoming passive. It's radical, conscious action, fuelled not by desire but by devotion. You are more engaged, more alive than ever before but with a fundamental shift in motivation that moves from "What will I get?" to "What can I give?" This is the only reliable secret to inner peace in a chaotic world.

'Thank you.'

Kannan received a standing ovation. Everyone present stood up to applaud this man's wisdom and his remarkable way with words. They stood as one, those who had met him and those who hadn't, each mesmerized by what Kannan had said, in awe of the possibilities on the way forward.

♦

As everyone in the audience shuffled out of the auditorium, Om, lost in his thoughts, started to pack up the sound-recording equipment. Even Aakash had thanked him profusely and left for a food delivery. Om, replaying parts of the speech in his mind, thought it was such a treat to listen to Kannan. He also remembered the first time he had met Kannan, many years ago.

It was merely three days after Om had pulled off an audacious cyber breach by hacking all laptops connected to the premier wireless network in the country. The news still featured in heated discussions across the nation. He had done what he wanted. Yet, he sulked as he sat in an abandoned fort near his house. His genius was proven yet the silence within him screamed louder than before. He believed nothing would change. Life would remain the same. The daily despair, struggle and helplessness would follow him to his grave.

He had chosen to hide in this decrepit fort—abandoned for years—because he felt nobody could track him here. Not digitally, not physically. Until he heard a voice nearby call out his name.

'Om! Om? I know you're in there. Come out,' a man's voice said.

Om panicked, thinking it was the police.

How could they find me? Om thought as he grabbed a stick for self-defence. The only exit was the entrance gate. No escape.

'I know you're scared but please come out. I just want to talk,' the voice said.

Om peeked out from behind a wall.

He saw a tall young man, wearing an ivory kurta, with dark flowing hair and eyes glittering like emeralds. Om understood this man was not from the police.

'Who are you?' Om enquired from behind the wall.

'I am Kannan. May we speak face to face?' Kannan asked in a soothing tone.

Om emerged, wary but curious. Kannan did not seem like a threat.

'How did you find me?' Om asked.

'How did you hack the laptops? Like you, I too have some secrets, my friend,' Kannan said with a playful smile.

'I saw your video on TV, Om, and honestly it made me angry,' Kannan said.

'Of course, it did. How dare someone like me, an untouchable, hold the nation to ransom? Yet I did,' Om said in an angry tone.

'No, my friend. I wasn't angry at you. I was angry with our society for making you feel invisible. What you did was a cry for help. I understand that, but it actually helped me,' Kannan said.

'How is that?' Om asked curiously.

'You helped me to find my purpose. When I heard you speak, your pain helped me realize that I want to help others. Even if I don't succeed, I want to know I tried,' Kannan replied.

'How can you help me? I did something big but still I am here, hiding in this abandoned fort with no clue about what's next,' Om said, visibly frustrated.

'What if I tell you what's next?' Kannan said, with a smile lacing his face.

Om looked at Kannan, puzzled.

'Come work with me. I shall pay you well. I want to build my personal team and I can use your skills. Rest assured there will be no discrimination. Your caste won't define you. I will also never tell the police but protect you,' Kannan said.

'You are trying to lure me out. This is a trap,' Om said suspiciously.

'You are speaking from passion. Hear this.'

yayā dharmam adharmaṁ cha kāryaṁ chākāryam eva cha
ayathāvat prajānāti buddhiḥ sā pārtha rājasī

Chapter 18, Verse 31

'Do you know what this means?' Kannan asked Om.

Om paused, then translated Kannan's words. 'When the intellect is clouded by passion, it struggles to discern between right and wrong, good and evil.'

Kannan nodded. After a moment of silence, Om decided to accept the offer. 'I'll do it,' he replied.

'But why would you want to hire me? I'm a criminal,' Om persisted.

Kannan smiled. 'Because together, my friend, we will grow!' he said simply.

yatra yogeshvaraḥ kṛiṣhṇo yatra pārtho dhanur-dharaḥ
tatra śhrīr vijayo bhūtir dhruvā nītir matir mama

Chapter 18, Verse 78

Wherever Lord Krishna, the master of all Yog, and Arjuna, the greatest archer, are present, there will undoubtedly be everlasting abundance, success, prosperity, and virtue.
I am absolutely convinced of this.

Author's Note

**Surrender and trust the process.
The journey begins here.**

When I first picked up the Bhagavad Gita, I wasn't seeking enlightenment. Only clarity. Life then felt noisy, restless and far too fast. On some days, I didn't even want to live. Yes, I felt heavy and low.

Like many of you, I was balancing ambition with anxiety, independence with uncertainty. I didn't know If I could achieve what I wanted. I was disturbed, unsettled by my circumstances and honestly, lost—trying to follow the 'right' path in life.

I could have never imagined at that point that an ancient scripture could directly speak to my inner chaos and address the mayhem.

But it did.

And that was the beginning.

This book is not just a tribute to what the Shree Bhagavad Gita has done for me—it is a reflection of my own transformation. It took me five years to write, not because I lacked the words, but because I needed time. Time to unlearn. Time to sit quietly in the company of these verses and not just to read them. Time to seek out the wisdom of *yogi*s, scholars and *pandit*s. And most importantly, time to observe how this book could transform the lives of those around me.

Every story in this book is real in spirit, even if the names and settings are fictional. Every character, even Kannan, lives the Gita in their own way. Yet one singular truth echoes throughout the Gita—it is not a book just for scholars, it is for everyone. It won't solve your problems but it will teach you to see them differently.

And perhaps that's all we ever really need.

I am certain I could not have done this alone, without the support of all those who have contributed generously along the way.

To my parents, Mr Arun and Mrs Sheeba Bansal, and my grandparents, Mr Bisan Lal and Mrs Prem Bansal—thank you for never binding me with expectations or outcomes. That freedom was a realization and a lesson I learnt only after reading the Gita.

I would like to thank my husband, Mr Aabhas Gugnani, and our family. Aabhas, thank you for being my constant pillar. Without you, none of this would have been possible. Your support and quiet encouragement have helped me to believe in myself, just because you never stopped believing in me.

To my sister, Aanchal—thank you for being there right from the start. You took time out, went through every chapter with me, and helped shape this book when I needed it the most. And my brother, Swayam, for being the light of our lives.

While the Shree Bhagavad Gita is my real *guru*, my mentor Mr Yogesh Chordia has been instrumental in shaping my journey. Thank you for your support, which has been unwavering and unconditional. You selflessly worked to help map out my path without ever seeking anything in return. For me, you have been a true *yogi*.

To Mr Anand Pillai—thank you for helping me understand by patiently guiding me through the verses and showing me how to live them. You often say you did little, but to me, it is who you are that made all the difference. Your selflessness was a lesson by itself. And to Monish, who introduced us, I am forever grateful.

To Mr Shyam Sundar Pandit ji—thank you for helping me through an entire chapter of the Gita which I struggled to understand. Thank you for your time, generosity and wisdom.

I would also like to thank the entire Rupa team, who have worked with me on this book with such care and sensitivity, especially during the final stages.

And to all those whose names may not appear here, but whose presence, support, or influence has quietly shaped this book—you know who you are. You will always hold a special place in my heart.

There are two individuals who have deeply shaped my thinking, and influenced who I am, though I've never met them—Mr Ratan Tata and Dr A.P.J. Abdul Kalam. While I wish I had the honour of meeting them, their lives and values continue to inspire me.

And finally, you, dear Reader. If you've reached this page, thank you. Thank you for trusting these stories, and in some way, for trusting me. I hope these chapters stirred something within you—a question, a stillness, a seed.

May you return to these verses whenever life feels uncertain. And remember—*Kannan* is not outside of you. He never was.

With humility and love.

—Aakriti Bansal